Collins Revision

KS3

Maths

Revision Guide

Levels 3–6

Keith Gordon

Revision contents

Workbook contents

NUMBER Place value

Hundreds, tens and units

- **Place value** is the value of a digit in a number depending on its **position** in the number. The number 562 is 500 + 60 + 2, so in columns it is:

Hundreds	Tens	Units
5	6	2

Top Tip!

You can say 500 or 100 for the value of the 5. 500 is better.

Example: Write the number 2057 in words.
Two thousand and fifty-seven.

Example: Here are 4 number cards.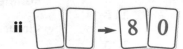

a What is the smallest even number you can make with the cards?
b What is the largest odd number you can make with the cards?
c Use two of the cards to make numbers as close as possible to the numbers below. The first one has been done for you.

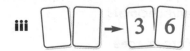

i 4 9 → 5 0   **ii** ☐☐ → 8 0   **iii** ☐☐ → 3 6

a 2498   b 8429   c ii 82   iii 42

Top Tip!

The closest number could be bigger or smaller. Work out the difference between the numbers.

Decimals

- Numbers smaller than a unit are called **decimal fractions**.

  The **decimal point** separates the whole numbers from the decimal fractions.

  The number 17.34 is 10 + 7 + 0.3 + 0.04, so in columns it is:

Tens	Units	.	Tenths	Hundredths
1	7	.	3	4

Top Tip!

If you are giving an amount of money in pounds and pence always write down 2 decimal places. £3.6 for £3.60 will be marked wrong.

The number of digits after the decimal point is the number of **decimal places** the number has.

Example: Here are some cards.

a Use three of the cards to make a number between 2 and 3.

b Use four of the cards to make a number between 1.5 and 1.6.

a 2.1, 2.5 or 2.6   b 1.52 or 1.56

How many tenths are there in 1.3?

One tenth

Write the number 'two thousand and four' in figures.

2004

levels
3-4

Sample worked test questions

a Write a number that is bigger than one thousand but smaller than one thousand and fifty. Give your answer in figures.

b Write a one decimal place number that is bigger than zero but smaller than a half.

Answers
a Any number from 1001 to 1049.
b 0.1, 0.2, 0.3 or 0.4

Did You Know?

The Dewey Decimal Classification system, devised by Melvil Dewey in the 1870s, is used to classify library books.

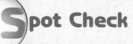

Spot Check

1 Write the numbers 1.3, 1.02, 1.2 and 1.324 in order with the smallest first.

2 | 3 | 6 | 4 | 5 | . |

Use the cards to

a write the biggest odd number you can

b write a three-digit even number bigger than 600

c write a number between 5 and 5.5

d write a number that is 10 times bigger than 0.36

Addition and subtraction

- You can use a **blank number line** or **column methods** for addition and subtraction.

Example: Work out 1056 + 309

```
        +300                    +9

1056                    1356   1365
```

So 1056 + 309 = 1365

Example: Work out 6523 – 670

```
   5  14  1
   6  5  2  3
–        6  7  0
   5  8  5  3
```

Top Tip!

If you use column methods make sure you line up the units column.
This type of question will be on Paper 1.
Always show the carry and borrowing digits.

Multiplication and division

- You can do short multiplication and division in columns or break it down into bits.

Example: Work out **a** 453 x 6 **b** 372 x 4

```
a       4  5  3        b   4 x 300 =  1 2 0 0
     x        6            4 x  70 =    2 8 0
     ───────────           4 x   2 =        8
     2 ₃7 ₁1  8                       ───────
                                      1 4 8 8
```

Example: Work out **a** 182 ÷ 7 **b** 655 ÷ 5

```
a                     b   600 ÷ 5 = 120
        2  6               50 ÷ 5 =  10
   7 ⟌ 1  8 ⁴2             5 ÷ 5 =    1
                                   ─────
                                     131
```

Top Tip!

The 1, 2, 5 and 10 times tables are fairly easy to remember. The 9 times table can be done using your fingers, e.g. 4 x 9. Hold your hands up and fold down the fourth finger.

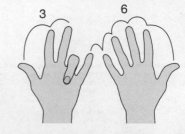

There are 3 fingers before the folded finger and 6 after it. 4 x 9 = 36

Spot Check

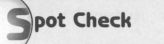

1 Work out
- **a** 632 + 24
- **b** 9970 – 880
- **c** 7 x 82
- **d** 8 x 67
- **e** 312 ÷ 6
- **f** 884 ÷ 5

level
4

Sample mental 💡 test questions

What is the remainder when 37 is divided by 8?

4 x 8 = 32, so 37 = 4 x 8 + 5. The remainder is 5.

What is 6 x 35?

6 x 30 = 180, 6 x 5 = 30, 180 + 30 = 210

Sample worked 💡 test question

Look at the sign for a car park.

Car Park
35p for 15 minutes

How much does it cost to park for an hour?

Answer
There are lots of ways to do these calculations but always show your method.
There are 4 lots of 15 minutes in one hour so the calculation is 4 x 35.

$$4 \times 30 = 120$$
$$4 \times 5 = 20$$
$$\overline{4 \times 35 = 140}$$

So it costs 140p or £1.40 to park for one hour.

Did You Know?

The word 'divide' comes from the Latin *dividere* which means to force apart.

The word 'multiply' comes from the Latin *multiplicare* which means to multiply.

NUMBER · Decimals

Ordering decimals

- When you put decimals in order, first compare the whole numbers, then the tenths, then the hundredths and then the thousandths.

Example: Which is bigger 1.24 or 1.6?

Compare 1.24 and 1.60.
1.60 is greater than 1.24.

Top Tip!
Give both numbers the same number of decimal places by adding zeros.

Example: Freddy, Mary and Alice are members of a family.
Freddy is 1.36 metres tall.
Mary is 1.5 metres tall.
Alice is 0.98 metres tall.

a Put the children in order of size with the smallest first.

a Write all the heights with the same number of decimal places.
Freddy 1.36, Mary 1.50, Alice 0.98
The order of size is: Alice, Freddy, Mary.

b Another child, Ben, is 0.5 metres shorter than Freddy.
How tall is Ben?

b 1.36 − 0.5 = 0.86 metres

Adding and subtracting decimals

- Adding and subtracting decimals is just like normal addition and subtraction. All you have to do is **line up the decimal point**.

Example: 1.23 + 3.4

```
  1 . 2 3
+ 3 . 4 0
---------
  4 . 6 3
```

Example: 3.4 − 1.68

```
  ²3̶ . ¹³4̶ ¹0
− 1 . 6 8
-----------
  1 . 7 2
```

Top Tip!
Add zeros here to fill the columns.

Spot Check

1 Put the following decimals in order from the smallest to the largest: 2.3, 1.89, 0.645

2 Add 0.5 to 1.8

3 Subtract 1.8 from 5.2

Sample mental test question

What is 1.2 − 0.3?

Think of a number line and count backwards.

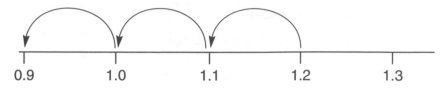

| 0.9 | 1.0 | 1.1 | 1.2 | 1.3 |

1.2 − 0.3 = 0.9

Sample worked test question

a Rick buys a cassette, a CD and a DVD.
How much does he pay altogether?

b What is the difference between the cost of a CD and a DVD?

 £3.99

 £9.49

 £15.35

Answers
Write the numbers in a column with the decimal points lined up.

a
```
    3 . 9 9
    9 . 4 9
+  15 . 3 5
  ─────────
  2 8 . 8 3
  1 1   2
```

He pays £28.83 altogether.

b
```
   14  12  1
  1⅚ . ⅗ 5
−   9 . 4 9
  ─────────
    5 . 8 6
```

The difference is £5.86.

Top Tip!

National Test questions usually put the question into a real-life situation.
This type of question will be on Paper 1.

Did You Know?
The first mathematician to use the idea of decimals was Aryabhata, who lived in India between 476 and AD 550.

NUMBER

Long multiplication and division

Long multiplication

- There are many ways of doing long multiplication. Two are shown here.

The **standard column** method.

Example: Work out 32 x 256

```
      2 5 6
  x     3 2
      5 1 2
+ 7 6 8 0
    8 1 9 2
```

The **box method**.

Example: Work out 43 x 264

X	200	60	4
40	8000	2400	160
3	600	180	12

Add up the numbers in the boxes.

```
  8 0 0 0
  2 4 0 0
    1 6 0
      6 0 0
      1 8 0
+       1 2
1 1 3 5 2
```

Top Tip!

Decide which method you prefer and stick with it.

Long division

- There are two ways of doing long division.

The **standard column** method.

Example: Work out 962 ÷ 37

```
        2 6
  37 | 9 6 2
    -  7 4
       2 2 2
    -  2 2 2
           0
```

The repeated subtraction or '**chunking**' method.

Example: Work out 896 ÷ 28

```
    8 9 6
  - 5 6 0    20 x 28
    3 3 6
  - 2 8 0    10 x 28
      5 6
  -   5 6     2 x 28
       0     32 x 28
```

Top Tip!

Some test questions usually ask part **a** as a long multiplication and part **b** as a long division and put the question into a real-life situation.

Top Tip!

Write out some of the easier times tables for the divisor:

```
 1 x 28 =  28
 2 x 28 =  56
 4 x 28 = 112
10 x 28 = 280
20 x 28 = 560
```

Subtract the biggest multiple you can each time.

 **Spot Check**

1 Work out 37 x 52

2 Work out 918 ÷ 17

Sample worked test question

a A garden centre has 576 winter pansies for sale.
Each plant costs 28p.
How much will all 576 cost?

b The pansies are packed in trays of 18.
How many trays does the garden centre have?

Answers

a *This is done by the box method.*
The total is £161.28.

X	500	70	6
20	10000	1400	120
8	4000	560	48

```
  1 0 0 0 0
    1 4 0 0
        1 2 0
    4 0 0 0
        5 6 0
+         4 8
  1 6 1 2 8
```

Top Tip!

Estimate the answer as a
check on your working:
28 x 576p
Round this to 30 x 600p
= 18 000p
= £180

b *This is done by the standard method.*
They have 32 trays.

```
        3 2
18 | 5 7 6
   −  5 4 0
        3 6
   −    3 6
          0
```

Top Tip!

Check an answer to a division by
multiplying by the original divisor:

18 x 32 =
10 x 30 = 300
10 x 2 = 20
 8 x 30 = 240
 8 x 2 = 16
          576

Did You Know?

The oldest surviving calculating
aid is the Salamis tablet
which was used in 300 BC.
It is now in the National
Museum in Athens.

NUMBER

Rounding and approximation

levels 3-4

Rounding to nearest 10, 100 etc.

- Most numbers used in everyday life are rounded. For example, the size of football crowds, the values of companies etc.

Example: Round the following numbers to **i** the nearest 10 **ii** the nearest 100

a 238 **b** 1945

a i 238 is 240 to the nearest 10 **ii** 200 to the nearest 100

b i 1945 is 1950 to the nearest 10 **ii** 1900 to the nearest 100

Top Tip!

If a number is halfway between two possible values, such as 45, then round upwards to 50.

levels 3-4

Rounding to decimal places

- The number of **decimal places** a number has is the **number of non-zero digits after the decimal point** (zeros directly after the point count).

  For example, 17.32 has 2 decimal places, 3.005 has 3 decimal places and 0.0802 has 4 decimal places.

Example: Round the following numbers to **i** 2 decimal places **ii** 1 decimal place

a 3.672 **b** 0.239

a i 3.672 is 3.67 to 2 decimal places **ii** 3.7 to 1 decimal place

b i 0.239 is 0.24 to 2 decimal places **ii** 0.2 to 1 decimal place

Top Tip!

When you have a decimal answer you don't have to round it off unless the question asks you to.

levels 3-4

Rounding to 1 significant figure

- The number of **significant figures** a number has is the **number of non-zero digits** (zeros between digits count as significant figures).

  For example, 1700 has 2 significant figures, 3005 has 4 significant figures and 0.08 has 1 significant figure.

- You only need to be able to round numbers to 1 significant figure.

Example: Round the following numbers to 1 significant figure.

a 2672 **b** 0.38 **c** 4.92 **d** 112

a 2672 is 3000

b 0.38 is 0.4

c 4.92 is 5

d 112 is 100

Top Tip!

The abbreviation for decimal places is d.p. and s.f. for significant figures.

 **S**pot Check   **1** Find approximate answers to **a** 178 × 32 **b** 306 ÷ 48

Approximations

- It is useful to be able to approximate the answer to calculations. This way you can check if your answers are correct.

Example: By rounding the numbers to 1 significant figure find an approximate answer to

$$\frac{312 \times 58.2}{19.3}$$

Rounding the numbers to 1 significant figure makes the calculation $\frac{300 \times 60}{20}$

20 goes into 60 three times so the calculation becomes $300 \times 3 = 900$

An approximate answer is 900.

Sample mental test question

The length of a piece of wood is given as 80 cm to the nearest 10 centimetres. What is the smallest possible length it could be?

To the nearest 10 the smallest length it could be is 75 cm.

Sample worked test question

The lengths of these rivers are shown in the following table.

River	Length (km)	To nearest 10 km	To nearest 100 km
Thames	346		
Shannon	323		
Severn	355		

a Complete each column.

b Another river is described as being 290 km to the nearest 10 km and 300 km to the nearest 100 km.

   i Could the river be 296 km in length?

   ii What is the shortest length it could be?

Answers

a

River	Length (km)	To nearest 10 km	To nearest 100 km
Thames	346	350	300
Shannon	323	320	300
Severn	355	360	400

b **i** No 296 would be 300 to the nearest 10

   ii 285 km

Did You Know? The longest river in the world is the Amazon, which is about 6500 km long.

NUMBER

Multiplying and dividing decimals

levels 3-4

Multiplying by powers of 10

- When you **multiply** by **10** all the digits move **one** place to the **left**. When you **multiply** by **100** all the digits move **two** places to the **left**.

Example: Work out **a** 2.79 x 10 **b** 3.2 x 100

a | Tens | Units | . | Tenths | Hundredths
| | 2 | . | 7 | 9

x 10 2 7 . 9

b | Hundreds | Tens | Units | . | Tenths | Hundredths
| | | 3 | . | 2

x 100 3 2 0 .

- You will need to add a zero in part **b** and you do not have to put in the decimal point for a whole number.

levels 3-4

Dividing by powers of 10

- When you **divide** by **10** all the digits move **one** place to the **right**. When you **divide** by **100** all the digits move **two** places to the **right**.

Example: Work out **a** 32.4 ÷ 10 **b** 2.7 ÷ 100

a | Tens | Units | . | Tenths | Hundredths
| 3 | 2 | . | 4

÷ 10 3 . 2 4

b | Units | . | Tenths | Hundredths | Thousands
| 2 | . | 7

÷ 100 0 . 0 2 7

- You will need to add a zero before and after the decimal point in part **b**.

Top Tip!
Remember it's the digits that move when multiplying, not the decimal point.

level 5

Multiplying and dividing decimals

- Multiplying and dividing decimals is just like normal multiplying and dividing. All you have to do is keep the decimal point lined up.
- The decimal point in the answer is always underneath the decimal point in the question.

Example: Work out 3.76 x 4

```
    3 . 7 6
  x       4
  1 5 . 0 4
    3   2
```

Example: Work out 8.04 ÷ 6

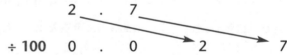

Top Tip!
Estimate the answer just to be sure.
3.76 x 4 is approximately 4 x 4 = 16
8.04 ÷ 6 is approximately 9 ÷ 6 = 1.5

A book costs £2.99. How much do 5 books cost?

5 lots of £3 are £15. £15 – 5p = £14.95

Divide 3.45 by 3.

Split the calculation:

(3 ÷ 3) + (0.45 ÷ 3) = 1 + 0.15 = 1.15

level
4

Sample worked test questions

a A shop sells boxes of chocolates for £3.38. How much do 10 boxes cost?

£3.38

b A box of 6 Easter eggs costs £16.20. How much does each egg cost?

£16.20

Answers

a *Move the digits one place to the left 3.38 x 10 = 33.8*
10 boxes will cost £33.80.

b
```
        2 . 7 0
   6 | 1 6 .⁴2 0
```
Each egg costs £2.70.

Top Tip!

Don't forget to put a zero on the end as the answer is in pounds and pence.

Top Tip!

Don't forget to estimate:
16.20 ÷ 6 ≈ 18 ÷ 6 = 3
'Is approximately equal to' can be shown by this symbol: ≈

Did You Know?

The world's most expensive Easter egg is the $24 million Fabergé Coronation Egg.

Spot Check   **1** Work out   **a** 0.7 x 100   **b** 4.52 ÷ 10   **c** 3.12 x 6   **d** 7.35 ÷ 5

Adding and subtracting negative numbers

Example: Work out +5 – 7

- Use a number line. Starting at zero, first move 5 units to the right, and then move 7 units to the left.

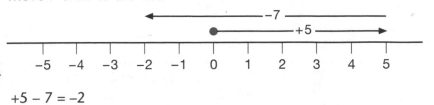

+5 – 7 = –2

> **Top Tip!**
> Always start at zero. Count to the **left** for **negative** numbers and to the **right** for **positive** numbers.

- Sometimes calculations have two plus or minus signs occurring together.

Example: Work out **a** –5 + –6 **b** –8 – –9

a
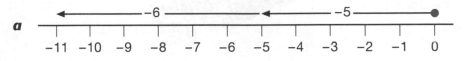

–5 + –6 = –11

b This is the same as –8 + 9.

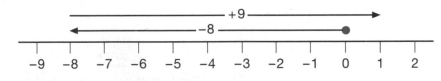

–8 – –9 = +1

> **Top Tip!**
> You must be very careful when two minus signs occur together. **Two minus** signs **together** act as a **plus**. So +8 – –5 is the same as +8 + 5 = 13.

Multiplying and dividing negative numbers

- Multiplying and dividing negative numbers is just like normal multiplying and dividing. All you have to do is combine the signs together correctly.

Example: Work out **a** –3 x +4 **b** –12 ÷ –2

- The rules for the signs are the same as above: + and – give a – answer; – and – give a + answer.

  a –3 x +4 is the same as – +3 x 4 = –12
  b –12 ÷ –2 is the same as – –12 ÷ 2 = +6

> **Top Tip!**
> When signs are **different** the answer will be **negative**. When signs are the **same** the answer will be **positive**.

Spot Check

1 Work out **a** –7 + –2 **b** +3 – –6 **c** –3 x –4 **d** +15 ÷ –3

What number is 5 less than –3?

As this is a mental question you will have to picture a number line in your head to get an answer of –8.

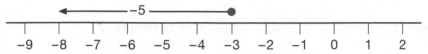

```
    ◄──────── –5 ─────────●
├────┼────┼────┼────┼────┼────┼────┼────┼────┼────┼────┤
-9   -8   -7   -6   -5   -4   -3   -2   -1   0    1    2
```

level
6

Sample worked 💡 test questions

1 The temperature at midnight in Edinburgh was –5 °C and at midday it was 7 °C.
By how many degrees did the temperature increase from midnight to midday?

2 You have these number cards.

-5   -3   -1   2   6

a Pick two cards to make the following calculations true.

i .... + ... = 5   **ii** .... – .... = –3   **iii** .... ÷ .... = –2

b Pick two cards to make the answer to the following as large as possible.

☐ X ☐ = ☐........

Answers

1 *From –5 to +7 is a difference of 12 °C.*

2 *Try different combinations of the cards.*
   a i *6 + –1 = 5* **ii** *–1 – 2 = –3* **iii** *6 ÷ –3 = –2*
   b *–5 x –3 = +15*

> **Top Tip!**
>
> Questions test if you understand the idea of negative numbers. Remember the rules!

Did You Know?

The lowest temperature recorded was –89.4 °C in Vostok, Russia, in 1983 and the highest was 59.4 °C in Libya in 1922.

NUMBER

Adding and subtracting fractions

levels
3-4

Cancelling fractions

- **Cancelling** fractions means looking for a **common factor** on the top and bottom of the fraction.
- Divide both the top number (**numerator**) and the bottom number (**denominator**) by the common factor.

  Once you've done this, the fraction is in its 'simplest form' or 'lowest terms'.

Example: Cancel the fraction $\frac{15}{20}$ to its simplest form.

15 and 20 have a highest common factor of 5.

$$\frac{15 \div 5}{20 \div 5} = \frac{3}{4}$$ We write this as: $\frac{{}^{3}\cancel{15}}{\cancel{20}_{4}}$

Top Tip!

Look for the largest number that divides into both the numerator and the denominator.

level
5

Adding fractions

- You can only add and subtract fractions if they have the same denominator.

Example: Add $\frac{2}{3} + \frac{3}{4}$

First, find the **lowest common multiple** of the two denominators, 3 and 4. The lowest common multiple is the smallest number in the 3 and 4 times table. This is 12.

Now make both fractions into twelfths.

$\frac{2}{3} = \frac{8}{12}$ (Multiply top and bottom by 4)

$\frac{3}{4} = \frac{9}{12}$ (Multiply top and bottom by 3)

Then just add the numerators and leave the denominator unchanged.

$$\frac{2}{3} + \frac{3}{4} = \frac{8}{12} + \frac{9}{12} = \frac{17}{12}$$

A fraction like $\frac{17}{12}$ is called **top heavy**. It can be made into a **mixed number** $1\frac{5}{12}$.

level
5

Subtracting fractions

Example: Subtract $\frac{5}{9} - \frac{1}{6}$

First, find the **lowest common multiple** of the two denominators, 9 and 6. The lowest common multiple is the smallest number in the 9 and 6 times table. This is 18.

Now make both fractions into eighteenths.

$\frac{5}{9} = \frac{10}{18}$ (Multiply top and bottom by 2)

$\frac{1}{6} = \frac{3}{18}$ (Multiply top and bottom by 3)

Then just subtract the numerators and leave the denominator unchanged.

Top Tip!

Subtracting a fraction from 1 is a common question e.g. $1 - \frac{11}{14} = \frac{3}{14}$

$$\frac{5}{9} - \frac{1}{6} = \frac{10}{18} - \frac{3}{18} = \frac{7}{18}$$

Write the fraction $\frac{4}{12}$ in its simplest form.

The common factor is 4, so divide top and bottom by 4 to get the answer of $\frac{1}{3}$.

Add a half and a quarter.

The fractions will be really easy, so you should know that

$\frac{1}{2} + \frac{1}{4} = \frac{3}{4}$

Sample worked  test question

A vegetable plot is planted with beans, peas, cabbages and carrots.

The peas take up $\frac{1}{4}$ of the plot.

The beans take up $\frac{3}{8}$ of the plot.

The cabbages take up $\frac{1}{6}$ of the plot.

How much of the plot is planted with carrots?

Answer

The total planted with peas, beans and cabbages is:

$\frac{1}{4} + \frac{3}{8} + \frac{1}{6}$

The common denominator is 24.

Making all the fractions into fractions with a denominator of 24 gives:

$\frac{6}{24} + \frac{9}{24} + \frac{4}{24} = \frac{19}{24}$

So $1 - \frac{19}{24} = \frac{5}{24}$ is planted with carrots.

level 5

Did You Know?

The population of the world increases by $2\frac{2}{3}$ people every second.

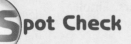

Spot Check

1 Cancel the following fractions to their simplest forms.

   a $\frac{15}{18}$ **b** $\frac{24}{28}$

2 Work out   **a** $\frac{3}{5} + \frac{1}{4}$ **b** $\frac{3}{4} - \frac{1}{6}$

Multiplying fractions

- Adding and subtracting fractions requires denominators to be the same but multiplying and dividing fractions is more straightforward.

Example: Multiply $\frac{2}{3} \times \frac{1}{4}$

When multiplying fractions, the new numerator is the product of the numerators and the new denominator is the product of the denominators.

Multiplying the numerators gives 2 x 1 = 2
Multiplying the denominators gives 3 x 4 = 12
So $\frac{2}{3} \times \frac{1}{4} = \frac{2}{12}$
This fraction $\frac{2}{12}$ will cancel to $\frac{1}{6}$.

To avoid problems with cancelling, cancel any fractions before multiplying:

$$\frac{\overset{1}{\cancel{2}}}{3} \times \frac{1}{\underset{2}{\cancel{4}}} = \frac{1}{6}$$

In this case, 2 on the top cancels with 4 on the bottom by a common factor of 2.

Example: Multiply $1\frac{1}{4} \times 1\frac{7}{15}$

Write both mixed numbers as **top-heavy** fractions, **cancel common factors** top and bottom and **multiply** the numerators and denominators. Finally, change the top-heavy answer back into a mixed number.

$$\frac{\overset{1}{\cancel{5}}}{\underset{2}{\cancel{4}}} \times \frac{\overset{11}{\cancel{22}}}{\underset{3}{\cancel{15}}} = \frac{11}{6} = 1\frac{5}{6}$$

Top Tip!

Always write mixed numbers as top-heavy fractions when multiplying or dividing.
$3\frac{3}{4} = \frac{15}{4}$ because there are 3 x 4 = 12 quarters in 3 plus the extra 3 quarters.

Dividing fractions

- When dividing fractions, turn the **second** fraction **upside down** and **multiply**.

Example: Divide $\frac{5}{6} \div \frac{1}{3}$

Write $\frac{5}{6} \div \frac{1}{3}$ as $\frac{5}{6} \times \frac{3}{1}$

Once again, cancel if you can. In this case, 3 and 6 cancel by a common factor of 3.

$$\frac{5}{\underset{2}{\cancel{6}}} \times \frac{\overset{1}{\cancel{3}}}{1} = \frac{5}{2} = 2\frac{1}{2}$$

Remember to change the top-heavy answer back into a mixed number.

Example: Divide $2\frac{1}{4} \div 1\frac{7}{8}$

Write both mixed numbers as **top-heavy** fractions before turning the **second upside down** and **multiplying**. Then cancel common factors top and bottom and multiply the numerators and denominators. Finally, change the top-heavy answer back into a mixed number.

$$\frac{9}{4} \div \frac{15}{8} = \frac{\overset{3}{\cancel{9}}}{\cancel{4}} \times \frac{\overset{2}{\cancel{8}}}{\underset{5}{\cancel{15}}} = \frac{6}{5} = 1\frac{1}{5}$$

Top Tip!

Always cancel before multiplying the numerators and denominators. It makes the calculations much easier.

Sample mental test questions

What is half of one third?

The fractions will be really easy, so you should know that $\frac{1}{2} \times \frac{1}{3} = \frac{1}{6}$

How many fifths are there in 2?

There are 5 fifths in 1, so there are 10 fifths in 2.

level
6

Sample worked test question

Work out $3\frac{3}{4} \div \frac{5}{8}$

Answer

Write the calculation as $\frac{15}{4} \div \frac{5}{8}$

Now turn the second fraction upside down and multiply
Cancel where possible.

$$\frac{\overset{3}{\cancel{15}}}{\cancel{4}} \times \frac{\overset{2}{\cancel{8}}}{\cancel{5}} = \frac{6}{1}$$

The calculation is $3\frac{3}{4} \div \frac{5}{8} = 6$

Top Tip!

Any fraction with a denominator of 1 is a whole number.

Did You Know?

One mile in every five of the US motorway network has to be straight so that it can be used as an airstrip in emergencies.

Spot Check

1 Work out   **a** $\frac{5}{8} \times \frac{4}{15}$ **b** $2\frac{2}{3} \times 1\frac{1}{8}$

2 Work out   **a** $\frac{2}{9} \div \frac{8}{15}$ **b** $2\frac{4}{5} \div 2\frac{1}{10}$

Simple fractions and percentages

- You need to be able to recognise some simple fractions and percentages.

Example: In this pie chart **a** what fraction is blue **b** what percentage is red?

Favourite colours

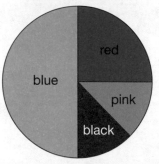

a Half ($\frac{1}{2}$) of the pie is labelled blue.

b A quarter is labelled red, so the percentage is 25%.

Top Tip!

The common percentages you should be able to recognise are:

25%   50%   75% $33\frac{1}{3}$% $66\frac{2}{3}$%.

These are the same as the fractions:

$\frac{1}{4}$ $\frac{1}{2}$ $\frac{3}{4}$ $\frac{1}{3}$ $\frac{2}{3}$

Fractions, percentages and decimals

- Fractions, percentages and decimals represent the **same value** and you should know the **equivalences** between them.

- You should know the following equivalences:

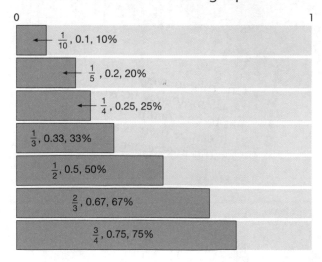

Example: Find the equivalent decimal and fraction to 40%.

$40\% = 2 \times 20\% = 2 \times \frac{1}{5} = \frac{2}{5}$

$= 2 \times 0.2 = 0.4$

Top Tip!

Use the known equivalences such as $10\% = \frac{1}{10} = 0.1$ to work out others such as 5% and 15%.

Example: Find the equivalent decimal and percentage to $\frac{4}{25}$.

$\frac{4}{25} = \frac{16}{100} = 16\%$

$16\% = 0.16$

Top Tip!

The decimal equivalent to a percentage is the percentage divided by 100.

What percentage is equivalent to the decimal 0.35?

As this is a mental question, you should be able to split the calculation:

0.35 = 3 x 0.1 + 0.05 = 30% + 5% = 35%.

Sample worked test question

The pie charts show the ages of people in a village and a town.

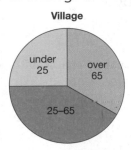

Village

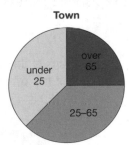

Town

a What percentage of the village are over 65?

b What percentage of the town are over 65?

c Tick the box that is true.

☐ There are more people over 65 in the village than the town.

☐ There are fewer people over 65 in the village than the town.

☐ There are equal numbers of people over 65 in the village and the town.

☐ You cannot tell how many people over 65 there are in the village and the town.

Explain your answer.

Answers

a 33% of the village are over 65.

b 25% of the town are over 65.

*c You cannot tell how many people are over 65 because the pie chart only shows the **proportions** and not the **actual numbers**. There may be more people in the town so 25% of a larger population may be more than 33% of a smaller population.*

Ensure you understand that pie charts only show proportions and not actual values.

Did You Know?

90% of people think that the American Thomas Edison invented the lightbulb. This isn't true. It was invented by Joseph Swan in Newcastle, England.

Spot Check

1 Fill in the missing equivalences in the table.

Decimal	Percentage	Fraction
0.15		
	35%	
		$\frac{9}{10}$

Percentage parts

- You should know that per cent means 'out of a hundred'.

Example: Work out **a** 15% of £45 **b** 32% of 75 kg

    a 10% of £45 is £4.50, so 5% of £45 is £2.25

       15% of £45 is £4.50 + £2.25 = £6.75

    b On the calculator, do 32 ÷ 100 x 75 = 24 kg or 0.32 x 75 = 24 kg.

Percentage increases and decreases

Example: A car's top speed is 125 mph. After a tune-up, its top speed increases by 12%. What is the new top speed?

Method 1

Work out 12% of 125.

12 ÷ 100 x 125 = 15

Add this to the original speed: 125 + 15 = 140 mph

Method 2

Use a **multiplier**. A 12% increase is a multiplier of 1.12.

1.12 x 125 = 140 mph

> **Top Tip!**
> Think of the **per cent** sign as '÷ 100' and the 'of' as a **times** sign. So 43% of 150 is 43 ÷ 100 x 150 = 64.5.

> **Top Tip!**
> Calculations are much easier if a 'multiplier' is used.
> 32% is a multiplier of 0.32.
> An increase of 15% is a multiplier of 1.15.
> A decrease of 8% is a multiplier of 0.92.
> Percentages are easily converted to decimals. Just divide by 100 (or move digits).

One quantity as a percentage of another

Example: What percentage is 42 out of 56?

The fraction is $\frac{42}{56}$.

This is divided to give the decimal: 42 ÷ 56 = 0.75.

This decimal is multiplied by 100 to give the percentage.

The whole calculation can be done as

42 ÷ 56 x 100 = 75%.

> **Top Tip!**
> If you divide the numerator by the denominator this gives the percentage multiplier:
> 42 ÷ 56 = 0.75, which is 75%.

Example: 17 students in a class of 25 stay for school dinners. What percentage is this?

The fraction is $\frac{17}{25}$.

Multiply the **numerator** (top number) by 4 and multiply the **denominator** (bottom number) by 4.

$$\frac{17 \times 4}{25 \times 4} = \frac{68}{100}$$

So the answer is 68%.

Sample mental test questions

What is 20% of £30?

Start by calculating 10%, which is £3, and then double it to £6.

In a test I got 16 out of 20. What percentage did I get?

Convert the denominator to 10 or 100.

16 out of 20 is the same as 8 out of 10, which is 80%.

Sample worked test question

30 students were asked how they travelled to school.

Transport	Boys	Girls
Walk	2	6
Bus	1	9
Car	2	7
Cycle	0	3
Total	5	25

a What percentage of boys come by bus?

b What percentage of girls walk to school?

c Misha said, 'Girls are healthier than boys because more of them walk to school'. Explain why she was wrong.

Answers

a 1 out of 5 is 20%.

b 6 out of 25 is $\frac{6}{25} = \frac{24}{100} = 24\%$.

c Although more girls walk than boys (6 compared to 2), the percentages are $\frac{2}{5} = 40\%$ for boys, and $\frac{6}{25} = 24\%$ for girls.

Top Tip!

Make the denominator into 100 by multiplying by a factor of 100 and do the same thing to the numerator.

Learn the factors of 100:

1 x 100
2 x 50
4 x 25
5 x 20
10 x 10

Did You Know?

In 1971 80% of 8 year olds walked to school. In 2001 the figure was just 7%.

Spot Check

1 Work out **a** £75 increased by 20%

  b 120 kg decreased by 12%

Ratio

- Ratio is a way of **comparing quantities**.
  For example, if there are 18 girls and 12 boys in a class, the ratio is 18 : 12.
  Because 18 and 12 have a **common factor** of 6, this can be cancelled down to 3 : 2.
  This is called the **simplest form**.

Example: Reduce the ratio 15 : 25 to its simplest form.
The highest common factor of 15 and 25 is 5.
Cancelling (dividing) both numbers by 5 gives 3 : 5.

- You may also be asked **direct proportion** questions.

Example: If 6 pencils cost £1.32, how much will 10 pencils cost?

Top Tip!
Use whichever method is easiest for the question. The unitary method is easier for this example because 6 : 132 is not an easy ratio to cancel.

Using **ratio**:
6 : 132 cancels to 1 : 22
Multiplying by 10 gives 10 : 220, so 10 pencils will cost £2.20.

Using the **unitary method**:
If 6 pencils cost £1.32, 1 pencil costs 1.32 ÷ 6 = £0.22
So 10 pencils cost 10 x £0.22 = £2.20.

These two methods are basically the same.

Calculating with ratio

- You need to be able to carry out different calculations involving ratios.

Example: If a family of 3 and a family of 2 had a meal and decided to split the bill of £35 between the two families, how much should each family pay?

It wouldn't be fair to split the bill in two, as there are more people in one of the families.
The bill should be split in the ratio 2 : 3.
The ratio 2 : 3 is a total of 2 + 3 = 5 shares.
Each share will be 35 ÷ 5 = 7.
2 x 7 = 14 and 3 x 7 = 21, so the £35 should be split as £14 and £21.

Top Tip!
Always check that the final ratios or values add up to the value you started with, e.g. 14 + 21 = 35.

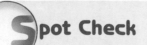
Spot Check

1 Write the ratio 14 : 18 in its simplest form.
2 Share £32 in the ratio 3 : 5.

Sample mental test questions

Look at the ratio 4 : 10. Write it in its simplest form.
The numbers will make finding a common factor easy.
In this case they cancel by 2 to give 2 : 5.

Divide £100 in the ratio 3 : 7.
The numbers will be easy to divide.
3 + 7 = 10, 100 ÷ 10 = 10, so the shares are £30 and £70.

level
6

Sample worked test question

Aunt Vera decides to give her nephews, Arnie, Barney and Clyde, £180.
The money is to be divided in the ratio of their ages.

Arnie is 1, Barney is 2 and Clyde is 3.

a　How much do they each receive?
b　The next year she decides to share another £180
　　between the three boys in the ratio of their ages.
　　How much do they each receive the following year?

Answers
a　*The total of their ages is 6, so divide 180 by 6.*
　　180 ÷ 6 = 30
　　Arnie gets 1 x 30 = £30.
　　Barney gets 2 x 30 = £60.
　　Clyde gets 3 x 30 = £90.

> **Top Tip!**
>
> Don't forget to check the totals:
> 30 + 60 + 90 = £180

b　*The following year the ages are 2, 3 and 4. This is a total of 9.*
　　180 ÷ 9 = 20
　　Arnie gets 2 x 20 = £40.
　　Barney gets 3 x 20 = £60.
　　Clyde gets 4 x 20 = £80.

Did You Know?

The 'Golden ratio', is about 1.618.
Leonardo Da Vinci used the
proportions of the Golden ratio in
the painting of the Mona Lisa.

ALGEBRA — Number patterns

level 4

Term-to-term rule

- A number pattern is a **sequence** or series of numbers that follow a **rule**.
- You should be able to say what the next two terms in this sequence are:

  3, 7, 11, 15, 19, ... , ...

  First look for the rule.

  In this case each number is 4 more than the previous number.

  This is called the **term-to-term rule**.

  So the next two numbers are 19 + 4 = 23 and 23 + 4 = 27.

- Sometimes the term-to-term rule is not so straightforward.

Example: Find the next two terms in this series of numbers and describe how the series is developed: 1, 3, 6, 10, 15, ... , ...

The next two terms are 21 and 28.

The series is built up by adding on 2, 3, 4, etc.

- The series 1, 3, 6, 10, 15, ... is a special series called the **triangle numbers** because the numbers can be made into triangle patterns.

Top Tip!

If you are asked to describe how a pattern builds up, say 'It goes up by 4 each time'.

Top Tip!

A good way of remembering the triangle numbers is to think of snooker and ten-pin bowling. Snooker has 15 red balls in a triangle and ten-pin bowling has 10 pins in a triangle.

level 6

The nth term of a sequence

- Sequences can also be described using algebraic rules.

Example: The nth term of a sequence is given by $2n - 1$.

Write down the first five terms of the sequence.

Substitute $n = 1, 2, 3, 4$ and 5 into the rule.

$n = 1$ gives $2 \times 1 - 1 = 1$

$n = 2$ gives $2 \times 2 - 1 = 3$

$n = 3$ gives $2 \times 3 - 1 = 5$

$n = 4$ gives $2 \times 4 - 1 = 7$

$n = 5$ gives $2 \times 5 - 1 = 9$

So the sequence is: 1, 3, 5, 7, 9, ... which are the odd numbers.

Top Tip!

The nth term is useful for finding out a number in a sequence without writing out all the sequence.

- There is a quick way of finding out the nth term.

Example: Find the nth term of the sequence: 4, 9, 14, 19, 24, 29, ...

What does each term go up by? In this case, 5.

The nth term will start $5n$.

What do you do to go from 5 to the first number, 4?

In this case, minus 1.

The nth term will be $5n$ minus 1 or $5n - 1$.

Example: Find the nth term of the sequence: 4, 7, 10, 13, 16, ...

The terms increase in steps of 3.

$3 + 1 = 4$, so the nth term is $3n + 1$.

I start at 5 and count down in equal steps: 5, 2, −1. What is the next number in the sequence?

First decide on the step. In this case, it is subtract 3.

Minus 1 subtract 3 is minus 4, so the answer is −4.

The nth term of a sequence is $(n + 2)^2$.

What is the 4th term of the sequence?

Substitute 4 for n:

$(4 + 2)^2 = 6^2 = 36$

The following patterns are made up of black and white hexagons.

Pattern 1   Pattern 2   Pattern 3   Pattern 4

Complete this table.

Pattern	Black hexagons	White hexagons
5		
10		
n		

Answers

The fifth pattern has 5 black hexagons and 11 white hexagons.
You should realise that the number of black hexagons is the
same as the pattern number and the number of white
hexagons is double the pattern number plus 1.

So the table is:

Pattern	Black hexagons	White hexagons
5	5	11
10	10	21
n	n	$2n + 1$

Top Tip!

Write out the sequence of numbers as a
list. This will help you to see the nth term:
Black hexagons: 1 2 3 4 5
So the nth term is n.
White hexagons: 3 5 7 9 11
So the nth term is $2n + 1$.

Did You Know?

The Fibonacci sequence 1, 1, 2, 3, 5, 8,
13 … is where each term is formed by
the sum of the two preceding numbers.
This sequence can be found in nature,
for example, in seed heads, flower petals
and sea shells.

Spot Check

1 What is the next term in the sequence: 3, 7, 11, 15, 19, …

2 What is the nth term of the sequence: 4, 8, 12, 16, 20, …

3 What is the nth term of the sequence: 5, 9, 13, 17, 21, …

ALGEBRA — Multiples, factors, square numbers and primes

Multiples and factors

- The **multiples** of a number are its **times table**. The **factors** of a number are the numbers that **divide exactly** into it. 1 and the number itself are always factors.

Example: Write down the first five multiples of 15.
The first five numbers in the 15 times table are:
15, 30, 45, 60, 75, …

Example: Find the factors of 24.
Look for all the products of whole numbers that make 24:
1 x 24, 2 x 12, 3 x 8, 4 x 6
The factors of 24 are: {1, 2, 3, 4, 6, 8, 12, 24}

> **Top Tip!**
> Factors come in pairs except for square numbers, where one number is its own 'pair':
> 2 x 2, 3 x 3, 4 x 4.

Square numbers

Example: Find the next two numbers in this series and describe how the series is built up:
1, 4, 9, 16, 25, … , …
The next two terms are 36 and 49.
The series is built up by adding on 3, 5, 7, 9, 11, and so on.

- Another way of spotting this series is to realise that each number can be written as: 1 x 1, 2 x 2, 3 x 3, 4 x 4, 5 x 5.
These numbers can be written using a special symbol called **square** or the **power 2** as: $1^2, 2^2, 3^2, 4^2, 5^2$.

> **Top Tip!**
> 3^2 is spoken as 'three squared'.

> **Top Tip!**
> The series 1, 4, 9, 16, 25, … is a special series called the **square numbers** because the numbers can be made into square patterns:

Square roots

- The opposite of square is **square root** which is shown by the symbol $\sqrt{81}$.

Example: **a** Find $\sqrt{81}$ **b** The value of x if $x^2 = 36$
a $\sqrt{81} = 9$ because 9 x 9 = 81
b $x = 6$ or -6 because 6 x 6 = 36 and -6 x -6 = 36

> **Top Tip!**
> Square roots are usually taken as positive but the solution to $x^2 = 36$ has two possible answers: ± 6 (plus or minus 6).

Prime numbers

- Numbers that only have two factors (1 and itself) are called **prime numbers**.

  There is no pattern to the prime numbers, you just have to learn them or work them out. The prime numbers up to 50 are:

  2, 3, 5, 7, 11, 13, 17, 19, 23, 29, 31, 37, 41, 43, 47

Top Tip!

2 is the only even prime number.

Sample mental test question

x squared is 36. What are the possible values of $2 + x$?

First, x must be +6 or –6, so $2 + 6 = 8$ and $2 + -6 = -4$

So there are two answers: 8 and –4.

Sample worked test questions

a Circle the numbers below that are factors of 60.

5   10   15   20   25   30
35   40   45   50   55   60

b Solve the equation
$x^2 - 4 = 60$

c From the list below write down:
i a square number   **ii** a multiple of 7   **iii** a prime number
13 15 17 19 21 23
25 27 29 31 33 35

Did You Know?

Each square centimetre of your skin has about 100 000 bacteria on it.

Answers
a   The numbers that divide into 60 are 5, 10, 15, 20, 30 and 60.
b x^2 must equal 64, so $x = 8$ or –8.
*c   **i**   The only square number in the list is 25.*
*   **ii** There are two multiples of 7 in the list: 21 and 35.*
*   **iii** There are several prime numbers in the list. Choose any from 13, 17, 19, 23, 29 or 31.*

Spot Check

1 From the list below write down:
  a a square number   **b** a prime number
  c a multiple of 4   **d** a multiple of 3 and 7
    3   6   9   12   15   18   21

ALGEBRA — Basic algebra

level 4

Simplifying expressions

- **Algebra** uses **letters** to **represent values** in equations, expressions and identities.
  You need to be able to simplify and manipulate algebraic expressions.

Example: Simplify **a** $2a + 3a$ **b** $3 \times 4a$ **c** $4a \times 5b$ **d** $2a \times 3a$
e $3a + 5b + 4a - 3b$ **f** $6a + 4 + 2a + 3$

a $2a + 3a = 5a$
b $3 \times 4a = 12a$
c $4a \times 5b = 20ab$
d $2a \times 3a = 6a^2$
e $3a + 5b + 4a - 3b = 7a + 2b$
f $6a + 4 + 2a + 3 = 8a + 7$

Top Tip!

$3a = 3 \times a$
The 'x' sign is assumed between a number and a letter.
Also $\frac{a}{3} = a \div 3$

level 4

Substituting numbers

- You need to be able to substitute numbers into expressions to find a value.

Example: If $a = 3$, $b = 4$ and $c = 7$, find the value of:
a $a + b$ **b** $2a$ **c** $4c - 5$ **d** $a^2 + b^2$ **e** $a(b + c)$

a $a + b = 3 + 4 = 7$
b $2a = 2 \times 3 = 6$
c $4c - 5 = 4 \times 7 - 5 = 23$
d $a^2 + b^2 = 3^2 + 4^2 = 3 \times 3 + 4 \times 4 = 25$
e $a(b + c) = 3(4 + 7) = 3 \times 11 = 33$

Top Tip!

Replace the letters by the numbers before doing the calculation.
Don't try to do it in your head:
If $a = 2$, $b = 6$,
$a + b = 2 + 6 = 8$
$2a = 2 \times 2 = 4$
$b^2 = 6^2 = 36$

levels 4-5

Interpreting expressions

- You need to be able to interpret expressions.

Example: Imran is x years old. His sister Aisha is 3 years older.
His brother Mushtaq is twice as old as Imran.

a How old is Aisha?
b How old is Mushtaq?
c What is the total of their three ages?

a Aisha is 3 years older than Imran so she is $x + 3$ years old.
b Mushtaq is twice as old as Imran so he is $2x$ years old.
c The total is $x + x + 3 + 2x = 4x + 3$ years.

Top Tip!

You cannot add together terms that contain different letters.
You cannot simplify $8a + 2b$.

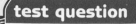

Sample mental test question

Look at the expression $2a + 5b + 6a - b$ and simplify it.

Combine the terms containing a, and then the terms containing b.
The answer is $8a + 4b$.

Top Tip!

A single letter on its own has a coefficient of 1, but there is no need to write it:
$1m = m$

level
4-5

Sample worked test question

There are n students in Form 9A.

a These expressions show how many students are in Forms 9A and 9B.
Write the number of students in 9C in words.

| 9A | n | students | |
| 9B | $n + 2$ | students | 2 more students than 9A |

| 9A | n | students | |
| 9C | $n - 3$ | students | .... |

b Two students move from Form 9A to Form 9B.
Write down the number of students in Forms 9A and 9B now.
9A has .... students. 9B has .... students.

Answers

a *9C has 3 fewer students than 9A.*

b *Taking 2 from n gives $n - 2$ and adding 2 to $n + 2$ gives $n + 4$.*
9A has $n - 2$ students. 9B has $n + 4$ students.

Did You Know?

On August 21, 1965, Charlton Athletic's Keith Peacock became the first substitute to appear in the Football League.

Spot Check

1 Simplify **a** $4a + 3 - 2a + 1$ **b** $4b \times 5b$
2 If $x = 3$ and $y = 4$, work out **a** $4x + 5y$ **b** $x^2 + y^2$

ALGEBRA Formulae

Formulae in words

- A **formula** is a rule that changes one number into another.

Example: **a** How much would it cost to park for 4 hours?

b If the total is £2, for how many hours was the car parked?

CAR PARK

£1 plus 50p per hour

a To park for 4 hours would cost £1 + 4 x £0.50 = £3.

b If it cost £2 to park, the car was there for 2 hours.
In this case the rule changes the number of hours parking (the input) into the cost of parking (output).

Flow diagrams

Example: Look at the flow diagram below.

a If the input is 6, what is the output? **b** What is the input if the output is 21?

| INPUT | → | Multiply by 2 | → | Add 3 | → | OUTPUT |

a An input of 6 gives an output of 6 x 2 + 3 = 15.

b To find an input from an output **work backwards** through the flow diagram.
An output of 21 has an input of (21 – 3) ÷ 2 = 9.

> **Top Tip!**
>
> A flow diagram can be used to help solve equations:
> $$2x + 3 = 21$$
> $$x = 9$$
>

Example: To cook a turkey, use this formula:

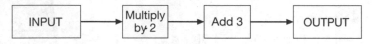

Cooking time (in min) = Weight of turkey (in kg) x 30 min + 30 min

a How long will it take to cook a 6 kilogram turkey?

b If a turkey took 5 hours to cook, how much did it weigh?

a Cooking time = 6 x 30 min plus 30 min
= 210 min = 3 hours and 30 min

b 5 hours = 300 min
Deduct 30 min: 300 – 30 = 270 min
Divide by 30: 270 ÷ 30 = 9
The turkey weighed 9 kilograms.

> **Top Tip!**
>
> Try to write the rule in symbols:
> $T = W \times 30 + 30$
> So, if $W = 6$,
> $T = 6 \times 30 + 30 = 210$

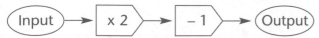
Look at the flow diagram. What is the input if the output is 7?

Input ➔ [x 2] ➔ [– 1] ➔ (Output)

*You should know to work **backwards** through the flow diagram: 7 + 1 = 8, 8 ÷ 2 = 4.*
The input is 4.

levels
4-5

Sample worked test question

The following rule can be used to prèdict the height of a boy when he is an adult.

Add 20 cm to the father's height (in cm).
Add the mother's height (in cm).
Divide by 2.
The boy's height will be within 10 cm of this height.

What will be the range of the adult height of a boy whose father is 174 cm tall and whose mother is 158 cm tall?

Answer
Add 20 cm to father's height: 174 + 20 = 194
Add the mother's height: 194 + 158 = 352
Divide by 2: 352 ÷ 2 = 176 cm
The boy's height will be between 166 cm and 186 cm.

Did You Know?

Toothpaste was first sold commercially in 1873 but the earliest formula for toothpaste was written in the fourth century. (It contained soot!)

Spot Check

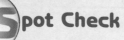

1 I think of a number, multiply it by 3 and subtract 4. The result is 17. What was the number I thought of?

2 Input ➔ [÷ 4] ➔ [+ 2] ➔ (Output)

What is the output if the input is 16?

Coordinates in the first quadrant

- **Coordinates** are used to describe the **position** of a point on a grid.

Example: A, B and C are three sides of a square.

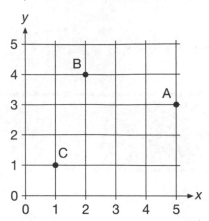

a Write down the coordinates of A, B and C.

b On the grid, plot D, the fourth corner of the square.

a A is (5, 3), B is (2, 4) and C is (1, 1).

b D should be plotted at the point (4, 0).

> **Top Tip!**
>
> There are two rules to remember. Start at the **origin** (0, 0) and move **horizontally** first, then **vertically** second.

Coordinates in all four quadrants

- **Negative coordinates** can also be used to describe the position of a point on a grid.

Example: A, B and C are three sides of a square.

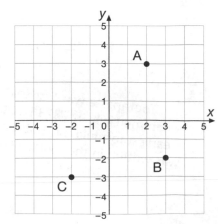

a Write down the coordinates of A, B and C.

b On the grid, plot D, the fourth corner of the square.

a A is (2, 3), B is (3, −2) and C is (−2, −3).

b D should be plotted at the point (−3, 2).

> **Top Tip!**
>
> Read the value from the *x*-axis first, and the value from the *y*-axis second.
>
> The point P is (−2, −3).

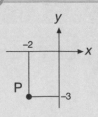

Look at the grid.

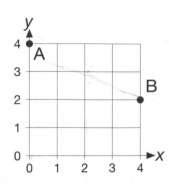

What are the coordinates of the midpoint AB?

The midpoint is (2, 3).

Sample worked **test question**

The graph shows the line $y = 2x$.

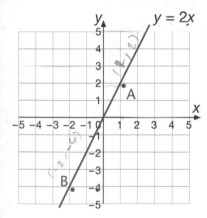

a Write down the coordinates of the points A and B.

b The point C (–8, –16) is on the line.
   Explain how you know this is true.

Answers

a *A is (1, 2) and B is (–2, –4)*

b *The y-value is twice the x-value.*
   2 x –8 = –16

Did You Know?

All Ordnance Survey maps are based on a coordinate grid. The origin is a point to the south-west of the Isles of Scilly.

 **Spot Check**

1 A is the point (6, –2) and B is the point (4, –2). What are the coordinates of the point halfway between A and B?

2 Which axis should you always read first?

Drawing graphs

Drawing graphs by plotting points

- Graphs show the relationship between variables on a coordinate grid.

  For example, the equation $y = 2x + 1$ shows a relationship between x and y where the y-value is 2 times the x-value plus 1.

  If $x = 0$, $y = 2 \times 0 + 1 = 1$. This can be represented by the coordinates (0, 1).

- Similarly, when $x = 1$, $y = 2 \times 1 + 1 = 3$. This is the point (1, 3).

  Other coordinates connecting x and y are (–3, –5), (–1, –1), (2, 5), etc.

  When these are plotted on a graph, they can be joined by a straight line.

- Coordinates are always given in the order: (x, y).

Example: Draw the graph of $y = 3x - 1$.

First find some points by choosing x-values:

Let $x = 0$, $y = 3 \times 0 - 1 = -1$

Let $x = 1$, $y = 3 \times 1 - 1 = 2$

Let $x = 2$, $y = 3 \times 2 - 1 = 5$

Let $x = -1$, $y = 3 \times -1 - 1 = -4$

Plot the points and join them up.

Top Tip!

Always label graphs.

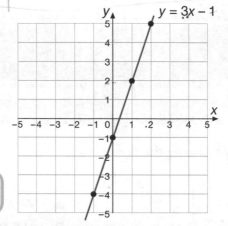

Drawing graphs by the gradient intercept method

- In an equation like $y = mx + c$, c is where the graph crosses the y-axis and m is the gradient.

  So for $y = 3x - 1$, the graph crosses the y-axis at –1 and has a gradient of 3. This means for every 1 unit across, the graph goes up by 3 units.

Example: Draw the graph of $y = 2x - 1$.

Start by plotting the point (0, –1).

Then from (0, –1) count 1 square across and 2 squares up, mark a point, repeat from this point and so on. You can also count 1 square back and 2 squares down.

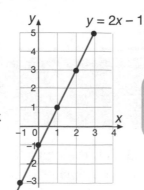

Top Tip!

Remember to read the x-axis first then the y-axis.

Sample mental test question

Look at the equation $y = 3x + 2$.

What is the value of y when $x = 2$?

Substitute $x = 2$ into the equation, so $y = 3 \times 2 + 2 = 8$

Sample worked test question

A is the point (2, 4).
B is the point (–4, –2).

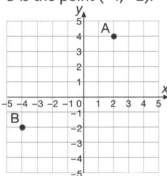

Which of the following equations is the graph of the straight line through A and B?

$$y = 2x \quad y = x + 2 \quad y = -2x \quad y = \frac{x}{2}$$

Explain your answer.

Top Tip!

Substitute the x- and y-values into the equations for all the pairs of coordinates you are given.

Answer

The equation is $y = x + 2$. This is the only equation that fits both A and B.

For A: $4 = 2 + 2$

For B: $-2 = -4 + 2$

Did You Know?

Nobody knows why x and y are used as the main letters in algebra, but x is now taken to represent something 'unknown', e.g. the X-files!

Spot Check

1 Complete the table for $y = 3x - 2$ for values of x from –2 to +4.

x	–2	–1	0	1	2	3	4
y	–8						10

x and y lines

- There are some graphs that you need to learn.

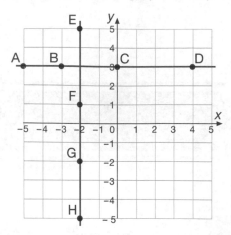

Top Tip!

All lines of the form $y = b$ are horizontal, and lines of the form $x = a$ are vertical.

Top Tip!

The x-axis is the line $y = 0$.
The y-axis is the line $x = 0$.

- The coordinates of the points A, B, C and D are (–5, 3), (–3, 3), (0, 3), (4, 3) respectively.

  You can see that they all have a y-coordinate of 3 and form a straight line on the grid.

  This line has an equation $y = 3$.

- The coordinates of the points E, F, G and H on the graph above are (–2, 5), (–2, 1), (–2, –2), (–2, –5) respectively.

  You can see that they all have an x-coordinate of –2 and form a straight line on the grid.

  This line has an equation $x = -2$.

x and y graphs

- Two other graphs that you need to know are:

$y = x$ $y = -x$

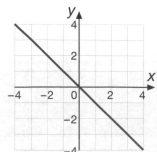

$x + y = c$ graphs

- The coordinates of the points A, B, C and D are (–3, 5), (0, 2), (3, –1), (5, –3) respectively.

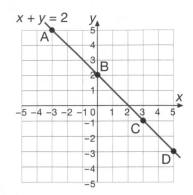

$x + y = 2$

You can see that the x- and y-coordinates add up to a total of 2. This line has an equation $x + y = 2$.

Top Tip!

All lines of the form $x + y = c$ slope at 45° from top left to bottom right, and pass through the value c on both axes.

Sample worked test question

The graph shows a triangle.

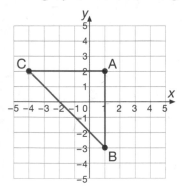

a What is the equation of the line through A and B? $x = 1$
b What is the equation of the line through A and C? $y = 4$
c What is the equation of the line through B and C? $y + x = -2$

Answers

a $x = 1$. AB is a vertical line through 1 on the x-axis.
b $y = 2$. AC is a horizontal line through 2 on the y-axis.
c $x + y = -2$. The line passes through (0, –2) and (–2, 0).

Did YOU Know?

René Descartes devised x- and y-coordinates in the seventeenth century. The grid is also called the Cartesian plane after Descartes.

Spot Check

1 Give the equations of the lines A, B and C.

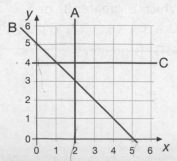

$x = 2$
$y = 4$
$x + y = 6$

BODMAS and powers

level
4

Order of operations

- To calculate 2 + 3 x 4, work out 3 x 4 first and then add this to 2 to give 14.
  This calculation uses the rules of mathematical operations, which is known as **BODMAS**.

- **BODMAS** stands for **B**rackets, **O**rder, **D**ivision, **M**ultiplication, **A**ddition, **S**ubtraction.
  This is the order in which operations must be done.
  For example:
  Brackets are always worked out first.
  Powers are always worked out before multiplication.

> **Top Tip!**
>
> **Order** is another name for **power**. In the National Tests, the powers will be **square** (power 2) or **cube** (power 3).

Example: Work out **a** 10 – 2 x 3 **b** (10 – 2) x 3

    a According to BODMAS, multiplication comes before subtraction, so find 2 x 3 first.

       The calculation is: 10 – 2 x 3 = 10 – 6 = 4.

    b BODMAS tells you to work out the bracket first.

       The calculation is: (10 – 2) x 3 = 8 x 3 = 24.

Example: Work out **a** $20 \div 4^2$ **b** $(20 \div 4)^2$

    a BODMAS tells you to work out the power (order) first, and then do the division.

       The calculation is: $20 \div 4^2 = 20 \div 16 = 1.25$ or $1\frac{1}{4}$.

    b BODMAS tells you to work out the bracket first, and then find the power.

       The calculation is: $(20 \div 4)^2 = 5^2 = 25$.

Example: Put brackets in the following calculations to make them true:

    a 3 + 4 x 5 – 1 = 28 **b** $3 + 2^2 + 6 = 31$

    a As the calculation is written it works out as 3 + 4 x 5 – 1 = 3 + 20 – 1 = 22.

       By trying out brackets we can see that (3 + 4) x (5 – 1) = 7 x 4 = 28.

    b As the calculation is written it works out as $3 + 2^2 + 6 = 3 + 4 + 6 = 13$.

       By trying out brackets we can see that $(3 + 2)^2 + 6 = 5^2 + 6 = 25 + 6 = 31$.

levels
4-5

Powers

- You have already met the powers 2 (square) and 3 (cube). Powers are a short way of writing repeated multiplications so $3^4 = 3 \times 3 \times 3 \times 3 = 81$, $2^5 = 2 \times 2 \times 2 \times 2 \times 2 = 32$.

Example: Which is greater 3^5 or 5^3?

    $3^5 = 3 \times 3 \times 3 \times 3 \times 3 = 243$, $5^3 = 5 \times 5 \times 5 = 125$

    So 3^5 is greater.

> **Top Tip!**
>
> You should know the squares of all the numbers up to 15^2 and the cubes of 1, 2, 3, 4, 5, and 10.

Sample mental test question

Look at the expression $3m^2$.

What is the value of the expression when $m = 10$?

Using BODMAS, $3m^2 = 3 \times m^2 = 3 \times 10^2 = 3 \times 100 = 300$.

Sample worked test questions

a   Write the answers to:
  i $(5 + 3) \times 4$ **ii** $5 + (3 \times 4)$

b   Work out the answer to: $(8 - 3) \times (4^2 \div 2)$

c   **i** Put brackets in the calculation to make the answer correct:
  $16 \div 2 + 6 \times 4 = 8$

  ii Put brackets in the calculation to make the answer correct:
  $16 \div 2 + 6 \times 4 = 56$

Answers

a   *Using the rules of BODMAS the answers are:*
  i $8 \times 4 = 32$ **ii** $5 + 12 = 17$

b   *Work out the brackets first. Within the second bracket, the power should be calculated first.*
  $(8 - 3) \times (4^2 \div 2) = 5 \times (16 \div 2) = 5 \times 8 = 40$

c   *Trying brackets in various places gives:*
  i $16 \div (2 + 6) \times 4 = 16 \div 8 \times 4 = 2 \times 4 = 8$
  ii $(16 \div 2 + 6) \times 4 = (8 + 6) \times 4 = 14 \times 4 = 56$

Did You Know?

The only two words with the vowels used once and in order are 'abstemious' and 'facetious'.

Spot Check

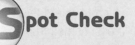

1 Work out   **a** $5 + 5^2 \div 10$ **b** $(5 + 5)^2 \div 10$

2 Put brackets in this calculation to make it true: $9 + 6 \div 3 + 5 = 10$

ALGEBRA — Equations 1

Basic equations

- 'I am thinking of a number. I double it and add 6. The answer is 12. What was the number I thought of?'

  This type of question can usually be solved in your head to give the answer 3.

- It can also be written as an **equation**.

  An equation is an expression involving a certain letter, x say, that is equal to a number.

  '**Solving the equation**' means **finding** the **value** of x that makes it true.

Example: The puzzle above could be written as: $2x + 6 = 12$

To solve this equation, you need x on its own on the left-hand side of the equals sign. You do this by applying the **inverse operations** to **both sides**.
First, eliminate '+ 6' by doing the inverse operation '– 6':
$2x = 6$
Now eliminate 'x 2' by doing the inverse operation '÷ 2':
$x = 3$

Example: Solve **a** $\frac{x}{2} - 3 = 7$ **b** $\frac{x-3}{2} = 6$

a First add 3, then multiply by 2.
$\frac{x}{2} = 10$
$x = 20$

b First multiply by 2 and then add 3.
$x - 3 = 12$
$x = 15$

> **Top Tip!**
> There are different ways of writing the solution to an equation, but they all arrive at the same solution:
> $2x + 6 - 6 = 12 - 6$
> $2x = 6$
> $2x \div 2 = 6 \div 2$
> $x = 3$

Fractional equations

- A **fractional equation** is one in which the **variable** appears as the numerator or **denominator** of a fraction.

Example: Solve the equation $\frac{x}{2} = \frac{7}{4}$

The first step in solving a fractional equation is to **cross-multiply**. This means multiply the denominator of the left-hand side by the numerator of the right-hand side and multiply the denominator of the right-hand side by the numerator of the left-hand side.
So: $4 \times x = 2 \times 7$
Tidy up the terms: $4x = 14$
Solve the equation: $x = 3\frac{1}{2}$ or 3.5

> **Top Tip!**
> You could just write down $4x = 14$ and then solve the equation.
> Answers can be left as top-heavy fractions, such as $\frac{14}{4} = \frac{7}{2}$ unless you are asked for an answer in its **simplest form**.

Example: Solve the equation $\frac{2}{x} = \frac{7}{11}$

Cross-multiplying: $22 = 7x$
This equation has the x-term on the right so reverse the equation: $7x = 22$
Divide by 7: $x = \frac{22}{7} = 3\frac{1}{7}$

> **Top Tip!**
> You can remember cross-multiplying by thinking of
>
> $\frac{x}{2} \diagtimes \frac{7}{4}$
> which is where the term 'cross' comes from.

Sample mental 💡 test question

Look at the equation $3x - 4 = 11$.

What value of x makes the equation true?

If $3x - 4 = 11$, $3x = 15$ and $x = 5$.

Sample worked 💡 test question

Solve the equations to find the values of x, y and z.

$$3x + 10$$
$$\frac{y}{2} - 10 \longrightarrow = 40$$
$$z^2 + 4$$

Answers

$3x + 10 = 40 \Rightarrow 3x = 30 \Rightarrow x = 10$

$\frac{y}{2} - 10 = 40 \Rightarrow \frac{y}{2} = 50 \Rightarrow y = 100$

$z^2 + 4 = 40 \Rightarrow z^2 = 36 \Rightarrow z = 6 \;(or\; -6)$

Did You Know?

The world's largest jigsaw puzzle had 18240 pieces and took 10 months to solve.

🔍 Spot Check

1 Solve the equations **a** $3x - 8 = 10$ **b** $\frac{x}{4} = \frac{5}{2}$

2 Look at these cards.

| $2x - 5$ | $5x + 9$ | $3x + 7$ | $4x + 1$ |

Card A   Card B   Card C   Card D

a What value of x makes card A equal to 8?

b What value of x makes card B equal to 4?

c What value of x makes card C equal to 7?

d What value of x makes card D equal to 0?

Equations with brackets

- 'I am thinking of a number. I add 6 and double the answer. The final answer is 16. What was the number I thought of?'

- This problem can be written as an equation using **brackets**.

  If the number thought of is x, then the first action is to add 6 giving $x + 6$. This answer is doubled which is written as $2(x + 6)$. The brackets are essential. The final equation is $2(x + 6) = 16$.

Example: Solve the equations **a** $2(x + 6) = 16$ **b** $3(x - 5) = 12$

a To solve this equation, you need x on its own on the left-hand side of the equals sign. You do this by **multiplying out** the brackets to give $2x + 12 = 16$.

First, eliminate '+ 12' by doing the inverse operation '− 12':

$2x = 4$

Now eliminate 'x 2' by doing the inverse operation '÷ 2':

$x = 2$

b First expand the brackets, then add 15 and divide by 3:

$3x - 15 = 12$

$3x = 27$

$x = 9$

Top Tip!

There are different ways of writing the solution to an equation, but they all arrive at the same solution:

$2(x + 6) = 16$

$x + 6 = 8$ (divide by 2)

$x = 2$ (subtract 6)

Equations with the letter on both sides of the equals sign

Example: Solve $3x + 6 = x + 10$

To solve this you need to have x on its own on the left-hand side of the equals sign. To do this, move all the x terms to the left-hand side and all the number terms to the right-hand side.

When a term moves over the equals sign its sign (plus or minus) changes:

$3x - x = 10 - 6$

Now tidy up the terms: $2x = 4$

and solve the equation: $x = 2$

Example: Solve $4x + 7 = 2x + 21$

Rearranging: $4x - 2x = 21 - 7$

Tidying up: $2x = 14$

Solving: $x = 7$

Check

Left-hand side = $4 \times 7 + 7 = 35$ ✓

Right-hand side = $2 \times 7 + 21 = 35$ ✓

Top Tip!

Rearrange the equation before working anything out. If you try to rearrange and work out at the same time, you are likely to make a mistake.

Top Tip!

Always check your answer in the original equation.

Sample worked 💡 **test question**

Solve the equations

a $4s + 7 = s + 25$

b $12x + 30 = 6x + 33$

Answers

a Rearrange: $4s - s = 25 - 7$

$3s = 18$

$s = 6$

Check $4 \times 6 + 7 = 31$, $6 + 25 = 31$, so LHS = RHS

b Rearrange: $12x - 6x = 33 - 30$

$6x = 3$

$x = \frac{1}{2}$

Check $12 \times \frac{1}{2} + 30 = 36$, $6 \times \frac{1}{2} + 33 = 36$, so LHS = RHS

Top Tip!

Always check that the left-hand side = right-hand side
LHS = RHS

Did You Know?

The equals symbol (=) was first used by Robert Recorde (c. 1510–1558) in 1557.

Spot Check

1 Solve the equations   **a** $3(x - 8) = 15$ **b** $4x + 5 = 2x - 7$

2 Look at these cards.

| $2x - 1$ | $5x + 1$ | $3x + 7$ | $3x + 1$ |

Card A   Card B   Card C   Card D

   a What value of x makes card A equal to 8?

   b What value of x makes cards B and C equal?

   c Explain why there is no value of x that works for both cards C and D.

Trial and improvement

- The only way to solve an equation like $x^3 + 2x = 27$ is by **trial and improvement**.
- Trial and improvement is just sensible **guesswork**.

Example: There is a solution of the equation
$x^3 + 2x = 27$ between 2 and 3.
Find the solution to 1 decimal place.

Start by making a guess between 2 and 3:

2.5 is a sensible guess.	$2.5^3 + 2 \times 2.5 = 20.625$
Then make a better guess:	$2.6^3 + 2 \times 2.6 = 22.776$
Keep on making better guesses:	$2.7^3 + 2 \times 2.7 = 25.083$
	$2.8^3 + 2 \times 2.8 = 27.552$

When you find two 1 decimal place values that 'bracket' the answer, check the middle value to make sure which of the values is closer.

$2.75^3 + 2 \times 2.75 = 26.296\,875$

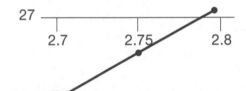

This means that 2.8 is the closer value to the answer.

Using a table to help you

- The best way to set out these problems is in a **table**. Tables are often given in National Test questions.

Example: Continue the table to solve the equation $x^3 - x = 50$

x	$x^3 - x$	Comment
4	60	Too high

First try the next number below 4, then keep on refining the guess.

x	$x^3 - x$	Comment
4	60	Too high
3	24	Too low
3.5	39.375	Too low
3.8	51.072	Too high
3.7	46.953	Too low
3.75	48.984375	Too low

The nearest 1 decimal place value is $x = 3.8$.

Sample worked test question

A rectangle has a side of length y centimetres.
The other side is of length $y + 3$ centimetres.

y cm
$y + 3$ cm

The area of the rectangle is 48.16 cm².
This equation shows the area of the rectangle:
$y(y + 3) = 48.16$
Find the value of y.

y	$y + 3$	$y(y + 3)$	Comment
4	7	28	Too low

Answer
The given starting value of 4 gives an area that is too low.

Continue the table with a higher value than 4.

y	$y + 3$	$y(y + 3)$	Comment
4	7	28	Too low
5	8	40	Too low
6	9	54	Too high
5.5	8.5	46.75	Too low
5.6	8.6	48.16	Exact

Because the answer is exact there is no need to test a halfway value.

Did You Know?
The longest trial in British history was the McLibel trial which lasted three years.

Spot Check

1 Show clearly why there is a solution of the equation
$2x^3 + 3x = 100$ between $x = 3$ and $x = 4$.

SHAPE, SPACE AND MEASURES

Scales

Reading scales

- Scales occur in everyday life and come in a variety of different forms. They may be round, as on a weighing machine, or straight as on a thermometer. It is important to be able to read scales accurately.

Example: Read the values from the following scales. Do not forget the units.

a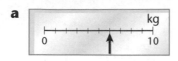

b **c** 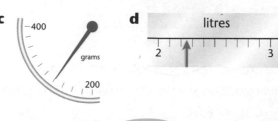 **d**

a 6 kg (the scale is marked in divisions of 1).

b 26 mph (the scale is marked in divisions of 2).

c 280 grams (the scale is marked in divisions of 20).

d 2.25 litres (the scale is marked in divisions of 0.1).

Top Tip!

Always check what each division represents. Also make sure which way the scale is reading. Normally scales read from left to right but some scales may read up, down, or right to left.

Timetables

- You should be able to read a clock face and a timetable.

Example: The timetable shows some times of the number 20 bus from Holmfirth to Penistone.

Holmfirth	Hade's Edge	Dunford Bridge	Victoria	Penistone
10:20	10:32	10:39	10:53	11:05
12:20	12:32	12:39	12:53	13:05
14:20	14:32	14:39	14:53	15:05

Top Tip!

Timetables always use the 24-hour clock. For example, 6 am is 06:00 and 1 pm is 13:00.

a How long is the journey from Holmfirth to Penistone?

b If I get to Dunford Bridge at 11:55 how long do I have to wait for a bus?

c John lives in Holmfirth and wants to catch a train in Penistone at 13:18.

  i Which bus should he catch?

  ii How long will he have in Penistone before the train leaves?

a All the buses take 45 minutes.

b 44 minutes. The next bus is at 12:39.

c **i** The 12:20 will get to Penistone at 13:05.

  ii 13 minutes from 13:05 to 13:18.

How many seconds are there in three minutes?

You should know that there are 60 seconds in one minute so there are 3 x 60 = 180 seconds in 3 minutes.

Sample worked **test question**

The clocks show the time that Kevin left his house and the time he returned.

a The digital clocks are showing the time in the 24-hour clock. How long was Kevin out of the house?

b Draw the time shown on the second digital clock on the ordinary clockface on the right.

Answers

a From 09:20 to 13:25 is 4 hours and 5 minutes.

b The time is 1.25 pm so the clock will show:

Did You Know?

Clocks in most jewellers' windows have their hands set to 10 to 2 so it looks like the clock is smiling.

**pot Check**

1 How long is there between 6.30 am and 14:05?

2 How much time has passed between the time on clock A and the time on clock B?

A  B

SHAPE, SPACE AND MEASURES

Metric units

levels 3-4

Length

- The basic unit of **length** is the **metre** (m).
- Other common units for length are the **kilometre** (km), **centimetre** (cm) and **millimetre** (mm).

  10 mm = 1 cm

  100 cm = 1 m $1 m = 1000 mm$

  1000 m = 1 km

Example: How many metres is 1.3 kilometres?

  1.3 km = 1.3 x 1000 = 1300 m

Example: How many centimetres is 54 millimetres?

  54 mm = 54 ÷ 10 = 5.4 cm

Top Tip!

2 metres is about the height of a normal doorway.

levels 3-4

Mass

- **Mass** is the correct term for **weight**.
- The basic unit of mass is the **kilogram** (kg).
- Other common units for mass are the **gram** (g) and **tonne** (T).

  1000 g = 1 kg

  1000 kg = 1 T

Example: How many kilograms is $2\frac{1}{2}$ tonnes?

  $2\frac{1}{2}$ T = $2\frac{1}{2}$ x 1000 = 2500 kg

Top Tip!

A normal bag of sugar weighs 1 kilogram. A 1p coin weighs $3\frac{1}{3}$ grams.

levels 3-4

Capacity

- **Capacity** is also known as **volume**.
- The basic unit of capacity is the **litre** (l).
- Other common units for capacity are the **millilitre** (ml) and **centilitre** (cl).

  1000 ml = 1 l

  100 cl = 1 l

Example: How many litres is 450 centilitres?

  450 cl = 450 ÷ 10 = 4.5 l

Top Tip!

A normal can of fizzy drink is about 330 ml or just over 3 cl.

How many metres is equivalent to 130 centimetres?

Divide by 100: 130 cm = 1.3 m

Learn what the prefixes mean:
milli- = ÷ 1000
centi- = ÷ 100
kilo- = x 1000

level
4

Sample worked test question

One large can and 4 small cans have a total mass of 4 kg.
The mass of the large can is 1.6 kg.
Each small can has the same mass.
What is the mass of one small can?
Give your answer in grams.

Answer
4 cans weigh 4 − 1.6 = 2.4 kg
1 can weighs 2.4 ÷ 4 = 0.6 kg
0.6 kg = 0.6 x 1000 = 600 g

Top Tip!

If converting from a **larger** unit to a **smaller** unit **multiply** by the conversion factor. If converting from a **smaller** unit to a **larger** unit **divide** by the conversion factor.

Did You Know?

The metre was originally defined as being one ten-millionth part of a quarter of the Earth's circumference.

Spot Check

1 Which unit would you use to **sensibly** measure the following:
   a the width of a pencil
   b the capacity of a tea cup
   c the length of a car journey.

2 Convert
   a 3.4 metres to centimetres
   b 4500 millilitres to litres
   c 5 tonnes to kilograms
   d 98 millimetres to centimetres

SHAPE, SPACE AND MEASURES

Imperial units

levels 3-4

Imperial units

- Britain is slowly changing from imperial units to metric units, but some imperial units are still used to talk about height and weight.

> I am 5ft 8in tall and weigh 11½ stone.

> I am 1.52m tall and weigh 45kg.

levels 3-4

Units of length, weight and capacity

- Here are some imperial units that are still in common use:

Length
12 in = 1 ft (foot)
3 ft = 1 yd (yard)

Weight
16 oz = 1 lb (pronounced 'pound')
14 lb = 1 st (stone)

Capacity
8 pints = 1 gallon

Top Tip!
You need to learn the approximations between imperial units and metric units. The symbol '≈' means 'is approximately equal to'.

levels 3-4

Conversion factors

- Here are some conversion factors that you need to know:

$1 \text{ m} \approx 3 \text{ ft}$ $1 \text{ in} \approx 2\frac{1}{2} \text{ cm}$ $1 \text{ kg} \approx 2\frac{1}{4} \text{ lb}$ $5 \text{ miles} \approx 8 \text{ km}$

$1 \text{ l} \approx 1\frac{3}{4} \text{ pints}$ $1 \text{ oz} \approx 30 \text{ g}$ $1 \text{ gallon} \approx 4\frac{1}{2} \text{ l}$

Example: Estimate the distance to the hotel in metres.

Sunbeach Hotel 600 yards

1 m ≈ 3 ft and this also means 1 m ≈ 1 yd.
So 600 yards is approximately 600 metres.

Top Tip!
Always check that your answers are sensible by relating them to your real-life experience.

Example: A man weighs $11\frac{1}{2}$ stone.

    a There are 14 lb in a stone.

      i How many pounds are there in $11\frac{1}{2}$ stone?

      ii Approximately how many kilograms is $11\frac{1}{2}$ stone?

    a i 11 stone = 11 × 14 = 154 lb and $\frac{1}{2}$ stone = 7 lb,
        so $11\frac{1}{2}$ stone = 161 lb.

    ii $161 \div 2\frac{1}{2} = 71.5$, so $11\frac{1}{2}$ stone ≈ 72 kg

Top Tip!
If converting to a **bigger** unit, **divide** by the conversion factor (kg are bigger than pounds), and if converting to a **smaller** unit, **multiply** by the conversion factor (cm are smaller than inches).

Sample worked  test question

 Dylan needs 8 gallons of petrol to fill the tank in his car.

How much does he pay?

Answer
This has to be done in two steps.
Change 8 gallons into litres first:
1 gallon ≈ 4½ litres, so 8 gallons ≈ 36 litres.
Now work out the cost:
36 × 90p = 3240p = £32.40

Did You Know?

Imperial units were originally based on parts of the body, so an inch was the length of the top joint of a thumb. A foot is obvious!

 **Spot Check**

1 The baggage allowance on an airline is 20 kg. Will a case weighing 50 lb be within the allowance?
2 There are 12 inches in a foot.
   a How many inches is 5 ft 8 inches?
   b Approximately how many metres and centimetres are there in 5 ft 8 inches?

SHAPE, SPACE AND MEASURES

Measuring angles and bearings

levels 3-4

Measuring angles

- You need to know the names for the different types of angles:

An **acute angle** is between 0° and 90°.

A **right angle** is 90°.

An **obtuse angle** is between 90° and 180°.

A **straight line** is 180°.

A **reflex angle** is between 180° and 360°.

A **complete turn** is 360°.

Example: Measure the size of the acute angle.

Count the numbers round from 0° until you meet the second line of the angle. This acute angle is 55°.

Top Tip!
Remember to start from 0° and make sure the **centre** of the **protractor** is on the **point** of the angle.

level 6

Bearings

Example: Measure **i** the distance and **ii** the bearings of points A and B from the point O.

Scale 1 cm : 10 km

i First measure the distances OA and OB.

OA is 5 cm and OB is 3.5 cm.

This means that OA is 50 km and OB is 35 km.

ii Draw a North line and place a protractor with its centre at O and 0° along the North line.

Measure clockwise to find the bearings.
A is on a bearing of 100°.
B is on a bearing of 240°.

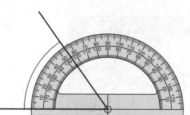

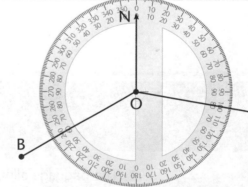

Top Tip!
A full round protractor is better for measuring bearings.

Top Tip!
Always start at **North** as zero degrees and measure **clockwise**. Bearings under 100° should be written with a zero in front e.g. 090°.

Look at the diagram.

Estimate the angle marked.

The angle is about 110°, so any answer from 100° to 120° would be an acceptable estimate.

Sample worked 💡 test question

Measure the size of each of the following angles.

a

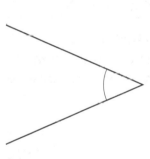

b

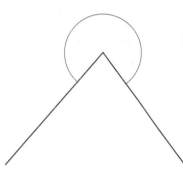

Answers
a *47°*
b *282°*

Did You Know?

The magnetic North Pole and the geographic North Pole are not the same place. They are about 3° apart if you are in Britain.

Spot Check

1 What is **a** an obtuse angle **b** a reflex angle?
2 What bearing is **a** East **b** South **c** West?

SHAPE, SPACE AND MEASURES

Angle facts

Angles on lines and around points

- You need to know how to use these angle facts:

  Angles on a **straight line** add up to 180°.

  Angles at a **point** add up to 360°.

Example: Find the angles marked x and y.

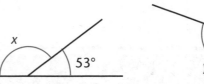

$x + 53 = 180$
$x = 180 - 53 = 127°$

$y + 115 + 90 = 360$
$y = 360 - 115 - 90 = 155°$

Angles in polygons

- You need to know some angle facts about **polygons**.

The three **interior** angles in a **triangle** add up to 180°.
$a + b + c = 180°$

The four **interior** angles in a **quadrilateral** add up to 360°. $a + b + c + d = 360°$

The **exterior** angle of a triangle equals the **sum** of the **two opposite interior** angles. $a + b = c$

Special triangles

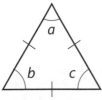 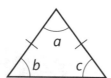 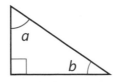

Equilateral triangle
$a = b = c = 60°$

Isosceles triangle
$b = c$

Right-angled
triangle $a + b = 90°$

Top Tip!

The small dashes marked on lines show that those lines are of the same length

Example: Find the angles marked with letters in these shapes.

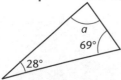 

$a + 28 + 69 = 180$
$a + 97 = 180$
$a = 180 - 97$
$a = 83°$

$b + 98 + 102 + 90 = 360$
$b + 290 = 360$
$b = 360 - 290$
$b = 70°$

angle on base = $180 - 110$
$= 70$
$c + 70 + 70 = 180$
$c = 40°$

levels
4-5

Sample worked 💡 test question

Find the size of the missing angles on each diagram.

a

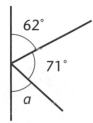

62°
71°
a

b

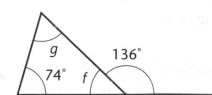

g
74°   f   136°

Top Tip!

Diagrams like these in tests are never drawn accurately so do not measure them with a protractor.

Answers

a   a + 62 + 71 = 180

   a + 133 = 180

   a = 47°

b   f + 136 = 180

   f = 44°

   g + 74 = 136

   g = 62°

Did You Know?

When mud dries in the sun, the cracks form curves that intersect at right angles.

Spot Check

1 What is the missing angle in this triangle?

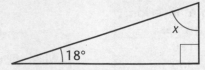

x
18°

2 Find the missing angles on this diagram.

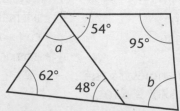

54°
a   95°
62°
48°   b

SHAPE, SPACE AND MEASURES

Angles in parallel lines and polygons

Intersecting lines and angles in parallel lines

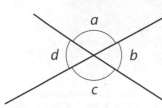

In these intersecting lines, vertically opposite angles are equal.

$a = c$ and $b = d$

- Parallel lines never meet. They provide some special types of angles.

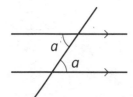

Alternate angles are **equal**.

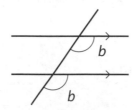

Corresponding angles are **equal**.

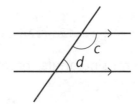

Interior angles add up to **180°**.

$c + d = 180°$

Example: Find the angles marked by letters.

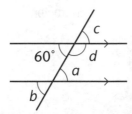

$a = 60°$ (alternate angle)

$b = 60°$ (vertically opposite angle to a)

$c = 60°$ (corresponding angle to a)

$d = 120°$ (interior angle to a)

Top Tip!

Alternate angles: look for a 'Z'.

Corresponding angles: look for an 'F'.

Interior angles: look for a 'C'.

Polygons

- Polygons are two-dimensional (**2-D**) shapes with **straight** sides.

Name of polygon	Number of sides	Sum of interior angles
Triangle	3	180°
Quadrilateral	4	360°
Pentagon	5	540°
Hexagon	6	720°
Heptagon	7	900°
Octagon	8	1080°

Top Tip!

When solving angle problems, always give a reason for how you found each angle.

Always use the correct mathematical words:
- alternate angles
- corresponding angles
- interior angles.

- A pentagon can be split into three triangles, so the sum of the five interior angles is $3 \times 180° = 540°$.

Regular polygons

• **Regular polygons** are polygons with **all sides equal** and **all angles equal**.

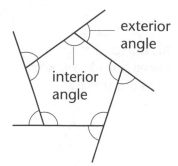

exterior angle

interior angle

The regular pentagon has five equal interior angles and five equal exterior angles.

Sum of the five exterior angles = 360°

So each exterior angle = 72°

Interior angle + exterior angle = 180°

Each interior angle = 108°

Sample worked test question

ABCD is a rectangle.

Find the angles marked with a letter.

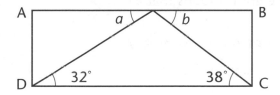

Answers

AB is parallel to CD, so a =32° (alternate angle)

and b = 38° (alternate angle).

Did You Know?

Islamic art is based on polygons, which can be constructed with circles.

Spot Check

1 Find the angles *a* and *b* in this regular hexagon.

2 Find the missing angles in this diagram.

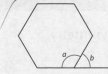

SHAPE, SPACE AND MEASURES

Symmetry

levels 3-4

Line symmetry

- With line symmetry, you can draw a line across a shape and both halves will fold exactly together.
- The line is called a **mirror line** or a **line of symmetry**.

Example: How many lines of symmetry have the following shapes?

Top Tip!

You can use a mirror or tracing paper to check for a line of symmetry.

     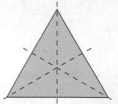

No lines of symmetry   1 line of symmetry   2 lines of symmetry   3 lines of symmetry

levels 3-4

Rotational symmetry

- With rotational symmetry, you can turn the shape into different positions that all look exactly the same.
- The number of different positions is called the **order of rotational symmetry**.

Example: What is the order of rotational symmetry for the following shapes?

Order 1   Order 2   Order 4   Order 8

Top Tip!

Rotational symmetry of order 1 is the same as saying 'no rotational symmetry'. You can give either answer.

Top Tip!

You can use tracing paper to check for rotational symmetry.

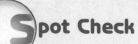 **S**pot Check

1 a How many lines of symmetry has this shape got?

b What is the order of rotational symmetry?

2 Write down the number of lines of symmetry of each of these shapes:

a   b   c

Quadrilaterals

Example: Write down the symmetry properties of these quadrilaterals.

Square

4 lines of symmetry
Rotational symmetry
of order 4

Rectangle

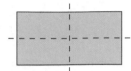

2 lines of symmetry
Rotational symmetry
of order 2

Parallelogram

0 lines of symmetry
Rotational symmetry
of order 2

Rhombus

2 lines of symmetry
Rotational symmetry
of order 2

Kite

1 line of symmetry
Rotational symmetry
of order 1

Trapezium

0 lines of symmetry
Rotational symmetry
of order 1

Sample mental test question

Look at the shape.
Complete the picture
so that the dotted line
is a line of symmetry.

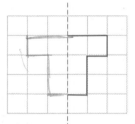

*Draw the other half
of the shape.*

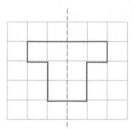

Sample worked test question

Shade three more squares so that the grid
has rotational symmetry of order 2.

Answer

Did You Know?

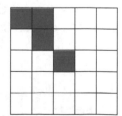

Palindromes are words or
phrases that read the
same backwards as
forwards, such as 'I prefer
pi' or 'Madam, I'm Adam'.

Reflections and rotations

level
5

Reflections

- A **reflection** creates a **mirror image** of a given object.

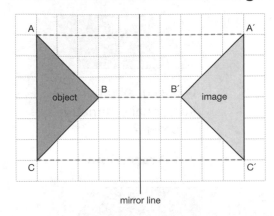

mirror line

- The object triangle ABC has been reflected in the mirror line to give the image triangle A'B'C'.

- The blue dashed lines show that any point on the object and its corresponding image point are the same distance from the mirror line. The line joining the two points also crosses the mirror line at right angles.

Top Tip!

If you trace the object and the image and fold along the mirror line,

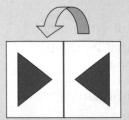

the two shapes should be exactly over each other.

level
5

Rotations

- A **rotation** turns the object through a given angle about a point called the **centre of rotation**.

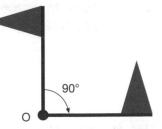

90°

O

- The flag has been rotated through 90° clockwise about the centre of rotation O.

Top Tip!

You can always use tracing paper to check your rotation.

Spot Check

1 Draw the reflection of the triangle in the dotted line.

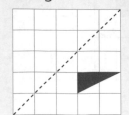

Top Tip!

Turn the page round so the mirror line is horizontal or vertical.
This makes it easier to see the reflection.

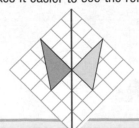

Congruency

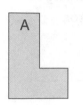

- In both reflections and rotations, the object and the image are **identical** in their **size** and **shape**. We say that the two shapes are **congruent**.

Example: Which two of the shapes below are congruent?

| A | B | C | D |

> **Top Tip!**
> **Congruent** means 'exactly the same shape and size'.
> **Similar** means 'the same shape but different sizes'.

B and D. A is the same shape as B but bigger. C is not the same shape. D is the same shape as B but rotated and reflected.

Sample mental test question

Look at the grid. Shape A has been rotated clockwise about the point O to make shape B.

What is the angle of rotation?

Using tracing paper, or just by looking, you can see that the angle of rotation is 90°.

Sample worked test questions

a Reflect the triangle in the mirror line.

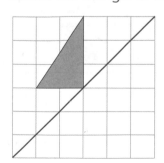

b Rectangle A has been rotated onto rectangle B about the point O. Describe the rotation.

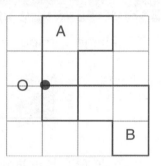

Answers

a

b *Rectangle A can move clockwise or anticlockwise, so there are two answers: a rotation of 90° anticlockwise or a rotation of 270° clockwise.*

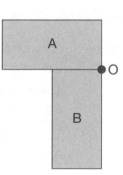

Did You Know?
The Earth rotates once every day. Venus rotates once every 243 Earth days. Nights on Venus can be very long!

SHAPE, SPACE AND MEASURES

Enlargements

level 6

Scale factor

- An **enlargement** changes the **size** of a shape.
- The **scale factor** tells you **how many times bigger** the shape is to be enlarged.
- The shape will stay the same but the sides will all increase by the same factor.

Example: Shapes B and C are enlargements of shape A. What is the scale factor of each enlargement?

Compare the lengths of any two common sides.
Shape B has a scale factor of $1\frac{1}{2}$.
Shape C has a scale factor of 2.

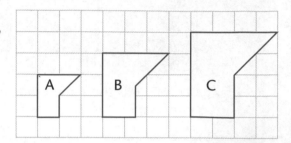

level 6

Centre of enlargement

- To enlarge a shape, you also need a **centre of enlargement**.

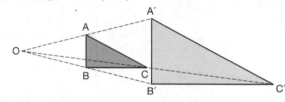

Triangle ABC is enlarged by a scale factor of 2 about the centre of enlargement O. All the sides are doubled in length.

$OA' = 2 \times OA$

$OB' = 2 \times OB$

$OC' = 2 \times OC$

Notice that all the measurements are from O.

Example: Enlarge the triangle ABC about the origin O by a scale factor of 3.

The coordinates of the vertices of triangle ABC are: A(3, 2), B(3, 1) and C(1, 1).

The coordinates of the vertices of triangle A'B'C' are: A'(9, 6), B'(9, 3) and C'(3, 3).

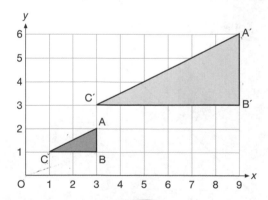

Top Tip!

If you draw lines through common vertices, they will meet at the centre of enlargement.

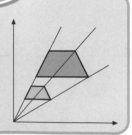

Top Tip!

The coordinates of the vertices of triangle ABC above are multiplied by the scale factor to give the vertices of triangle A'B'C'. This method works if the centre of enlargement is at the origin, but not if it is elsewhere.

Sample worked test question

Enlarge the trapezium ABCD by a scale factor of 2 about the origin O.

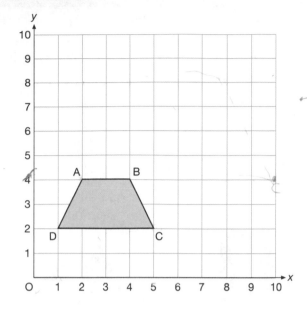

Answer

The coordinates of the enlarged trapezium A'B'C'D' are:

A'(4, 8), B'(8, 8), C'(10, 4) and D'(2, 4).

Did You Know?

If you place a sheet of paper on the floor and keep doubling the size of the pile, i.e. 1 sheet becomes 2, 2 sheets become 4 etc., after 50 doubles the pile will be 100 million kilometres high.

Spot Check

1 Enlarge this triangle by a scale factor of 3.

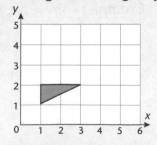

2 Triangle A has been enlarged to give triangle B. Find the scale factor and centre of enlargement.

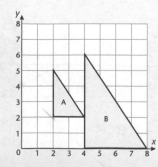

SHAPE, SPACE AND MEASURES

3-D shapes

Polyhedra

- **2-D** shapes are called **polygons** and **3-D** shapes are called **polyhedra**.
- These are the names of the 3-D shapes you need to know.

Cube

Cuboid

Square-based pyramid

Tetrahedron

Triangular prism

Cylinder

Cone

Sphere

- A **cuboid** has 12 **edges**, 8 **vertices** and 6 **faces**.

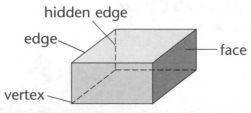

hidden edge

edge

face

vertex

Nets

- A **net** is a 2-D shape that can be folded to make a 3-D shape.

Example: This is a net for a square-based pyramid.

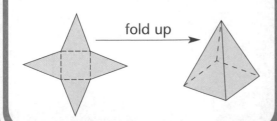

fold up

Plans and elevations

- A **plan** is a view of a 3-D shape **from above**.
- An **elevation** is a view of a 3-D shape from **one side**.

Example: These are the views for a triangular prism.

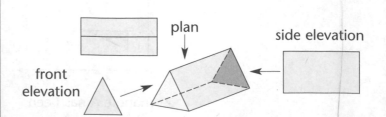

plan

side elevation

front elevation

Spot Check

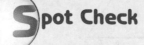

1 Which of the following are nets for a cube?

A   B   C   D

Isometric drawings

- 3-D shapes drawn on isometric paper are more accurate and measurements can be taken from the diagram.

Example: This is the isometric drawing for a cuboid:

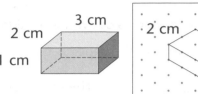

Top Tip!

When using isometric paper, the dots should form columns:

i.e.

not

Planes of symmetry

- A 3-D shape has **plane symmetry** if it can be **cut in half** so that one half is a **mirror image** of the other half.

Example: A cuboid has three planes of symmetry.

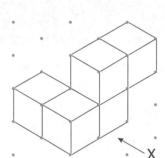

Sample worked test question

The diagram shows a shape made from 5 one centimetre cubes.
On the grid below draw:

a the plan **b** the elevation from X.

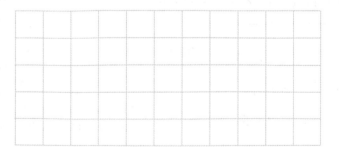

Answers

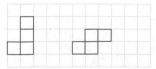

Did You Know?

Elevation is another term for height above sea level. Lake Titicaca is the highest lake in the world with an elevation of 3810 m. The Dead Sea is the lowest with an elevation of −411 m.

SHAPE, SPACE AND MEASURES
Perimeter and area

Perimeter

• **Perimeter** is the total **distance around** the outside of a 2-D shape.

Example: Find the perimeter of this shape.

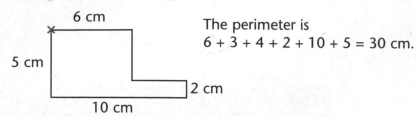

The perimeter is
6 + 3 + 4 + 2 + 10 + 5 = 30 cm.

Top Tip!
When finding a perimeter, put a mark on one vertex (corner) and count round the sides until you get back to the start.

Area

• **Area** is the **amount of space** inside a 2-D shape.

• The common units for area are: mm², cm² or m².

Area by counting squares

Example: Estimate the area of this shape.

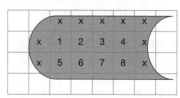

First count the number of whole squares. Then mark the squares where the area is more than half a square. An estimate for the area is $8 + 9 \times \frac{1}{2} = 12\frac{1}{2}$ cm².

Area of a rectangle

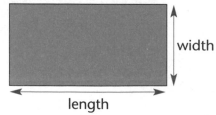

length

width

Example: Find the area of this rectangle.

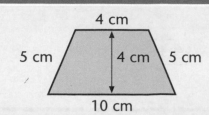

5 m

12 m

$A = lw = 12 \times 5 = 60$ m²

• Area = length x width
$A = l \times w$
$A = lw$

Top Tip!
Make sure you always write the correct units for area.

Spot Check

1 What is the perimeter and area of this shape?

4 cm

5 cm   4 cm   5 cm

10 cm

Area formulae

- In these formulae, *b* stands for 'base' and *h* stands for 'height' although the correct term is 'perpendicular height'.

Parallelogram

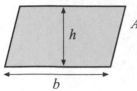

$A = bh$

Triangle

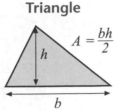

$A = \dfrac{bh}{2}$

Trapezium

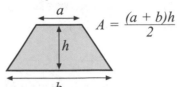

$A = \dfrac{(a + b)h}{2}$

Example: Find the area of these shapes.

a

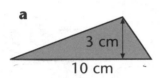

3 cm

10 cm

b

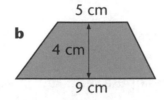

5 cm

4 cm

9 cm

a $A = \dfrac{bh}{2} = \dfrac{10 \times 3}{2} = 15$ cm²   **b** $A = \dfrac{(a + b)h}{2} = \dfrac{(9 + 5) \times 4}{2} = 28$ cm²

Top Tip!

Do not try to work these out in your head. Always substitute numbers into the formula. You will have more chance of reaching the correct answer.

Sample mental test question

A square has an area of 36 cm².
What is the perimeter of the square?

The length of a side of the square is 6 cm, since 6 x 6 = 36.
The perimeter of the square is 4 x 6 = 24 cm.

Sample worked test question

On a grid, draw a triangle that has an area of 6 cm².

Answer
Possible triangles are:

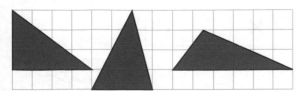

Did You Know?

On average there are about 4000 square metres of land for every person in Britain. That's less than a soccer pitch.

SHAPE, SPACE AND MEASURES

Circumference and area of a circle

Circumference of a circle

- The **circumference** is the **perimeter** of a circle.
- You need to know that $d = 2 \times r$.

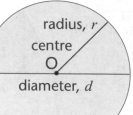

radius, r
centre
O
diameter, d

There are two formulae for the circumference of a circle:

- Circumference = 2 x π x radius

  $C = 2\pi r$

- Circumference = π x diameter

  $C = \pi d$

- π = 3.14 to 2 decimal places or use the π key on your calculator.

Example: Calculate the circumference of this circle.

8 cm

$C = \pi d = \pi \times 8 = 25.1$ cm (1 d.p.)

 Key sequence on your calculator: π × 8 =

Top Tip!

Always give your answer to 1 decimal place (1 d.p.) unless the question says otherwise.

Area of a circle

- Area = π x radius²

  $A = \pi \times r \times r$

  $A = \pi r^2$

Top Tip!

Questions will give either the radius or diameter. Make sure you use the correct value in the appropriate formula.

Example: Calculate the area of this circle.

7 cm

Top Tip!

Write down the formula first and always show your working.

$A = \pi r^2 = \pi \times 7^2 = 153.9$ cm² (1 d.p.)

 Key sequence on your calculator: π × 7 x² =

Top Tip!

Always square the radius before you multiply by π.

Sample worked test questions

a James' bike wheel has a radius of 30 cm. Calculate its circumference, giving your answer to the nearest centimetre.

b The circle and the square have the same area.

4 cm

x

Calculate x, the length of the side of the square.

a $r = 30$ cm , so $d = 60$ cm.
$C = \pi d = \pi \times 60 = 188$ cm (nearest cm)

b The area of the circle is $A = \pi r^2 = \pi \times 4^2 = 50.26...$
So $x = \sqrt{50.26...} = 7.1$ cm (1 d.p.)

Did You Know?

In early 2006 Chris Lyons from Australia recited the first 4400 digits of pi from memory.

 **Spot Check**

1 What is the circumference and area of this circle?

10 cm

2 A circular pond has a diameter of 6 metres.

A one metre path is built around the outside of the pond.

What is the area of the path?

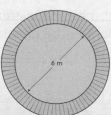

6 m

SHAPE, SPACE AND MEASURES

Volume

levels
3-4

Volume

- **Volume** is the **amount of space** inside a **3-D** shape.
- The common units for volume are: mm^3, cm^3 or m^3.

level
5

Volume of a cuboid

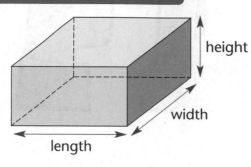

- Volume = length x width x height

$$V = l \text{ x } w \text{ x } h$$
$$V = lwh$$

Example: Find the volume of this cuboid.

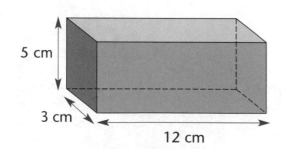

$V = lwh$

$= 12 \text{ x } 3 \text{ x } 5 = 180 \text{ cm}^3$.

Top Tip!

Substitute numbers into a formula before trying to work anything out.

level
6

Surface area of a cuboid

- There are 6 **faces** on a cuboid, with opposite faces having the same area.
- The **surface area** is given by

$$A = 2lw + 2lh + 2wh$$

Example: Find the surface area of the purple cuboid in the panel above.

$A = 2 \text{ x } 12 \text{ x } 3 + 2 \text{ x } 12 \text{ x } 5 + 2 \text{ x } 3 \text{ x } 5 = 72 + 120 + 30 = 222 \text{ cm}^2$.

Capacity

- **Capacity** is the **amount of space** inside a **hollow 3-D** shape.
- Capacity usually refers to the volume of a gas or liquid. You need to know 1000 cm³ = 1 litre.

Example: Find the volume of this fish tank, giving your answer in litres.

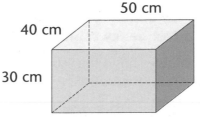

$V = 50 \times 40 \times 30$

$= 60\ 000$ cm³

$V = 60$ litres

Example: This is a net of a cuboid. If one square has an area of 1 cm², what is the volume of the cuboid?

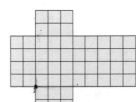

$V = 4 \times 3 \times 2 = 24$ cm³

Sample mental ☼ test question

The volume of a cube is 27 cm³.

What is the length of an edge of the cube?

Since 27 = 3 x 3 x 3, the length of an edge = 3 cm.

Sample worked ☼ test question

These two cuboids have the same volume.
Find the value of x.

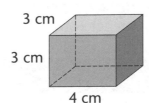

Answer

Volume of first cuboid = 36 cm³.

Volume of second cuboid = 6x = 36 cm³.

So x = 6 cm.

Did You Know?
The volume of the Sun can hold over a million Earths.

**pot Check**

1 What is the volume and surface area of this cuboid?

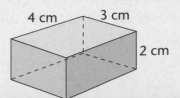

HANDLING DATA Statistics

Statistics

- Statistics involves collecting and interpreting **data**.
- Data is best collected by carrying out **surveys** or by using **questionnaires**.
- Data can be sorted easily by putting it into a table called a **tally chart** or a **frequency table**.

Example: This frequency table shows the scores when a dice has been thrown 30 times.

Score	Tally	Frequency
1	﹢﹢﹢﹢ │	6
2	﹢﹢﹢﹢	5
3	││││	3
4	﹢﹢﹢﹢ ││	7
5	﹢﹢﹢﹢	5
6	││││	4
	Total	30

Top Tip!

Note the tallies. Single marks are used for totals of 1 to 4 and a 'gate' is used for a total of 5.

Mode and range

- The **mode** for a set of data is the value that occurs **most often**.

  From the frequency table above, the score that occurs most often is 4. So we say the mode of the scores is 4 or the modal score is 4.

- The **range** for a set of data is calculated as: **the highest value – the lowest value.**

  From the frequency table, the range of the scores is 6 – 1 = 5.

Example: Find the mode and range of this data: 3, 5, 7, 4, 3, 2, 5, 8, 9, 10, 2, 3, 6, 4

  The value that occurs the most often (mode) is 3.
  The range is the difference between highest and lowest: 10 – 2 = 8.

Bar charts

- Data can be represented on various diagrams, such as a **bar chart**.
- When drawing a bar chart always remember to:
  - label the axes
  - leave gaps between the bars
  - write the values below the middle of each bar.

Example: This bar chart shows the scores on the dice for the frequency table above.

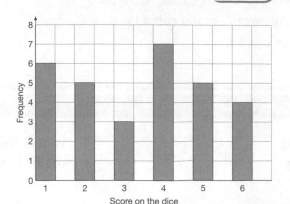

Look at the data shown: 5, 2, 10, 5, 5.

What is the range of the data?

The range is 10 – 2 = 8.

level
4

Sample worked test question

Here are the numbers of goals scored by a team in 20 games.

0 1 0 1 1 2 1 3 2 4

0 1 3 4 2 0 1 1 0 2

a Draw a frequency table to show the scores.

b What is the mode for the number of goals scored?

c What is the range of the number of goals scored?

Answers

a

Score	Tally	Frequency
0	卌	5
1	卌 ||	7
2						4
3				2
4				2
	Total	20

b *The mode is 1 goal.*

c *The range is 4 – 0 = 4 goals.*

Did You Know?

The average bed is home to over 6 billion dust mites.

Spot Check

1 Find the mode and range of the data shown in the bar chart. It shows the number of people in 10 cars.

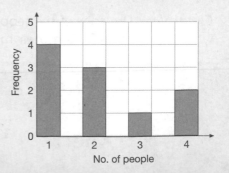

HANDLING DATA

Mode, median and mean

levels
3-4

The mode

- An **average** is a typical value for a set of data.
- The **mode** of a set of data is the value that occurs **most often**.

Example: Find the mode for this set of data.

10 13 14 10 13 10 15 16

The mode is 10.

Top Tip!

MOde = MOst common
Median = Medium (middle)
Mean = the 'nastiest' because it is the hardest to work out!

levels
3-4

The median

- To find the **median** for a set of data, first put the values in order from smallest to largest, and then pick out the exact **middle** value.

Example: Find the median for this set of data.

6 5 9 2 6 4 7 8 3

In order: 2 3 4 5 6 6 7 8 9

The median is 6.

Example: The ages of six people are: 21, 32, 25, 19, 23 and 18. Find their median age.

In order: 18 19 21 23 25 32

There are two numbers in the middle, so the median is the number halfway between 21 and 23. The median is 22.

Top Tip!

If data is not in order, it must be put in order.

levels
5-6

The mean

- To find the **mean** for a set of data, first find the **total** of all the **values** and then **divide** this total by the **number of values**.

The symbol for the mean is $\bar{x}$. $\quad \bar{x} = \dfrac{\text{Total of all values}}{\text{Number of values}}$

Example: The ages of six people are: 21, 32, 25, 19, 23 and 18. Find their mean age.

$\bar{x} = \dfrac{\text{Total of all values}}{\text{Number of values}} = \dfrac{138}{6} = 23$

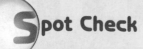 **Spot Check**

1 Find the mode, median and mean for this set of data.
19, 24, 24, 18, 22, 24, 27, 18

The mean and median from a frequency table

- To find the mean from a frequency table, add an extra column to find the total of all the values.

Example: The frequency table shows the marks for 20 students in a spelling test. Find the mean mark and the median mark.

Mark, x	Frequency, f	$x \times f$
5	1	5
6	0	0
7	3	21
8	5	40
9	8	72
10	3	30
Totals	20	168

$$\bar{x} = \frac{\text{Total of all values}}{\text{Number of values}} = \frac{168}{20} = 8.4 \text{ (mean)}$$

The median is between the 10th and 11th values. Counting up the frequency column gives 10th and 11th values as 9. Median = 9.

Top Tip!

If the mean is not an exact answer, then round it to 1 decimal place.

Sample mental test question

What is the mean of 19, 21, 23 and 37?

Add the numbers together: $19 + 21 + 23 + 37 = 100$ $\bar{x} = 100 \div 4 = 25$

Sample worked test question

a Find the mean of the numbers on these cards.

$$3 \quad 4 \quad 6 \quad 7$$

b Another card is added and the mean goes up by 2. What number is on the new card?

$$3 \quad 4 \quad 6 \quad 7 \quad ?$$

Answers

a The mean = $(3 + 4 + 6 + 7) \div 4 = 20 \div 4 = 5$

b The new mean is 7, so the five numbers add up to 35. The number on the new card is $35 - 20 = 15$.

Did You Know?

The average person in the UK spends 18 hours a week watching TV.

Comparing distributions

• You compare distributions in everyday situations, without even realising it.

Example: Two dinner ladies, Mary and Doris, serve chips in the school canteen.

mmm...
Chips!

Rajid went to Mary for his chips for a week. Mary gave out 18, 23, 25, 25, 34 chips.

The following week Rajid went to Doris for his chips. Doris gave out 23, 25, 27, 25, 25 chips.

Which dinner lady should Rajid go to to be given the most chips?

First, look at the averages and range:

	Mean	Median	Mode	Range
Mary	25	25	25	16
Doris	25	25	25	4

The averages are all the same but Mary's range is much larger than Doris'. So if Rajid caught Mary on a good day, he might have as many as 34 chips, but on a bad day he might have as few as 18. Doris is very consistent and will always give about 25 chips.

You could say, 'The averages are the same' and 'I would go to Mary as she has a bigger range and you might be lucky and get a lot of chips', or you could say, 'I would go to Doris because she has a smaller range and is more consistent'. It doesn't matter who you choose as long as you mention the **average** and the **range** and give **reasons** for your choice.

Top Tip!

The **range** measures the spread of the data so gives an indication of how **consistent** the data is.

Top Tip!

When comparing data using ranges and averages, you must **refer** to them both in your answer.

Example: John records the lateness of two school buses A and B.

Over a week, bus A is 0, 2, 5, 7 and 1 minute late.
Over the same week, bus B is 2, 4, 2, 4, 3 minutes late.

a Work out the mean and range for bus A.
b Work out the mean and range for bus B.
c Which bus is more reliable?
    Give reasons for your answer.

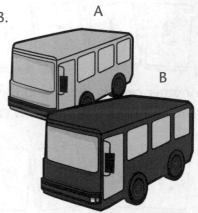

A

B

a Mean = (0 + 2 + 5 + 7 + 1) ÷ 5 = 15 ÷ 5 = 3 minutes
    Range = 7 − 0 = 7 minutes
b Mean = (2 + 4 + 2 + 4 + 3) ÷ 5 = 15 ÷ 5 = 3 minutes
    Range = 4 − 2 = 2 minutes
c Both buses have the same mean but bus B has a smaller range so is more consistent. Bus B is more reliable even though it is always late.

Top Tip!

Compare the averages, even if they are the same. Also compare the ranges.

Sample mental  test question

Give three numbers with a mode of 5 and a range of 2.

If there are three numbers and 5 is the mode, then two of the numbers must be 5. To give a range of 2, the other number must be 3 or 7. So there are two answers: 3, 5, 5 or 5, 5, 7.

Sample worked  test question

Jayne needs to pick an attacker for the netball team.
She looks at the scoring record of Asha and Rhoda.
In Asha's last five matches she scored 5, 7, 2, 9, 2 goals.
In Rhoda's last five matches she scored 5, 6, 5, 4, 5 goals.
Who should Jayne choose and why?

Answer
The averages for Asha are: Mode 2, Median 5, Mean 5.
The averages for Rhoda are: Mode 5, Median 5, Mean 5.
The range of Asha's scores is 9 – 2 = 7.
The range of Rhoda's scores is 6 – 4 = 2.
The averages are the same, except for the modes, but Rhoda has a smaller range so she is more consistent.
Although Asha may get a high score, she may also get a low score so Jayne should pick Rhoda.

Did You Know?

On an average work day, a typist's fingers travel 20 kilometres over a range of 20 cm.

 **pot Check**

1 Work out the mean and range of these two sets of data.
   a 4, 6, 6, 9, 10
   b 2, 5, 7, 8, 13

2/4/17

HANDLING DATA Line graphs

level 5

Plotting values

- A **line graph** is a clear way of showing **changes in data**.

Example: The maximum temperature in a town each month for a year is recorded.

	Jan	Feb	Mar	Apr	May	Jun	Jul	Aug	Sep	Oct	Nov	Dec
	4	9	13	19	25	28	32	29	22	17	13	7

a Which two months had a maximum temperature of 13 °C?

b Which was the hottest month?

c What is the difference between the hottest and coldest months?

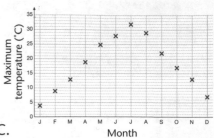

a Reading across from 13 °C on the *y*-axis gives the two months as March and November.

b July was the hottest month with a maximum temperature of 32 °C.

c January was the coldest month with a maximum temperature of 4 °C so the difference is 32 − 4 = 28 °C.

level 5

Trend lines

- You can see from the graph above that the temperature rises in summer. If we join the points, the lines between them have no meaning but they show the trend of the temperatures over the year.

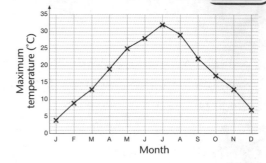

Example: The graph below shows Sam's height from the age of 2 to the age of 8.

a How many centimetres did Sam grow from the age of 2 to 8?

b Is it possible to estimate Sam's age at $3\frac{1}{2}$ years old?

a Sam was 54 cm at age 2 and 110 cm at age 8 so he grew 56 cm.

b Yes, growth is continuous so the line has a meaning this time. Sam was about 74 cm tall at age $3\frac{1}{2}$.

Example: The following graph shows the monthly gas use for the Henman family.

a During which month was the most gas used?

b During one of the months in the summer the Henman family went on holiday. Which month was this? Give a reason for your answer.

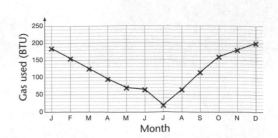

a The most gas was used during December as this is the highest value on the graph.

b July. The amount of gas drops dramatically in July suggesting that the family were not at home.

Sample worked 💡 **test question**

Jason records the temperature in his greenhouse once an hour. At 8 am it was 14 °C, at 9 am it was 20 °C, at 10 am it was 25 °C and at 11 am it was 29 °C.

This information is shown on the graph.

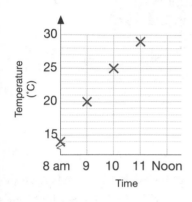

Top Tip!

You can **estimate** values from trend lines but you cannot say for sure what the values are.

a Estimate the temperature at 10.30 am.

b Explain why the graph cannot be used to predict the temperature at 12 noon.

Answers

a *Using the trend line between 10 am and 11 am, the temperature can be estimated as 27 °C.*

b *The trend line may not continue after 11 am. The sun could go in, or the windows could be opened.*

Did You Know?

The world's tallest person grew to a height of 270 cm.

 **pot Check**

1 The temperature drops by 4 °C from 5 am to 6 am. It was 7 °C at 5 am.

  a What was the approximate temperature at 5.30 am?

  b Can you estimate the temperature at 7 am?

2 Using the graph of Sam's height on the opposite page, decide during which years Sam grew the fastest. Explain how you can tell.

HANDLING DATA • Pie charts

Reading pie charts

- You need to be able to read and draw pie charts. The main thing to remember is that frequencies are represented by **angles** and that the **total frequency** will be equivalent to **360°**.

Example: This pie chart shows the favourite colours of Class 9A. If 5 students choose blue as their favourite colour, how many students are in Class 9A?

Favourite colours of Class 9A

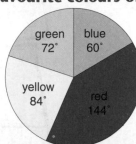

There are 5 students represented by 60°.

1 student is represented by 60 ÷ 5 = 12°.

There are 360° in the circle, and 360 ÷ 12 = 30.

There are 30 students, in the class.

Top Tip!

Always **label** pie charts and give a **title** to show what the pie chart represents.

Pie charts and frequencies

Example: This table shows the types of vehicles parked in a motorway service area.

Type of vehicle	Frequency
Car	40
Vans	22
Motorbikes	8
Lorries	20

Draw a pie chart to show the data.

First add up the frequencies: they total 90.

Divide this into 360 to find the angle that represents each vehicle: 360 ÷ 90 = 4°.

Now multiply each frequency by this figure. This is easily shown by adding another column to the table.

Type of vehicle	Frequency	Angle
Car	40	40 x 4 = 160°
Vans	22	22 x 4 = 88°
Motorbikes	8	8 x 4 = 32°
Lorries	20	20 x 4 = 80°

Then start with a circle, draw a radius and measure each angle in turn.

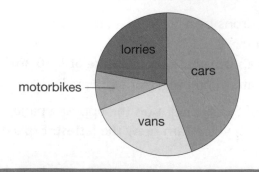

Top Tip!

It is useful to know the factors of 360:

1 x 360	8 x 45
2 x 180	9 x 40
3 x 120	10 x 36
4 x 90	12 x 30
5 x 72	15 x 24
6 x 60	18 x 20

The pie chart shows the ratio of men to women at a concert.

If 2000 people attended, how many women were there?

You can see from the pie chart that 75% of the people were women, 75% of 2000 = 1500.

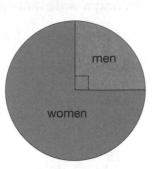

Sample worked test question

The pie chart shows the results of a survey about where families went for their holidays.

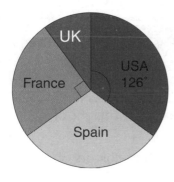

The sector for the USA represents 7 families.
How many families went to France?

Answer

There are 126° representing the USA sector.

7 families = 126°, so 1 family = 126 ÷ 7 = 18°.

There are 360 ÷ 18 = 20 families in the survey.

France is a quarter of the pie chart,
so 20 ÷ 4 = 5 families went to France.

Did You Know?

Every few years the village of Denby Dale in Yorkshire bakes a big meat pie. The last was the Millennium Pie in 2000 which was claimed to weigh 12 tonnes. However, nobody will admit to have seen it and the *Guinness Book of Records* doesn't recognise it.

Spot Check

1 If 7 out of 30 people prefer coffee, what angle would coffee have on a pie chart showing people's favourite drinks?

2 The 'dog' sector of a pie chart representing the favourite pets of a class has an angle of 20°.

   a Explain why there could not be 30 students in the class.

   b How many students could there have been in the class?

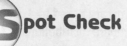

Grouped data

- When there is a lot of data covering a wide range, you may collect it using groups.

Example: This table shows the marks for Year 11 in their mathematics mock exam.

Mark, m	Frequency, f
$20 < m \le 30$	7
$30 < m \le 40$	29
$40 < m \le 50$	56
$50 < m \le 60$	32
$60 < m \le 70$	15
$70 < m \le 80$	8
$80 < m \le 90$	3

$20 < m \le 30$ means marks that are greater than 20 and less than, or equal to, 30.

- If you add up all the frequencies, you can tell that 150 students took the examination.

- However, you cannot tell exactly what any of the following are: the lowest mark, the highest mark, the mode, the median, the range or the exact mean.

Types of data

- **Continuous data** is data that can take **any value** with a **range**. For example, height of plants, weight of cattle and speed of cars.

- **Discrete data** is data that takes a **non-numerical** or **unique value**, such as colours of cars and shoe sizes.

Example: The diagram shows the speeds of 100 cars on the B1026 and 100 cars on the M1. Comment on the differences in the two distributions.

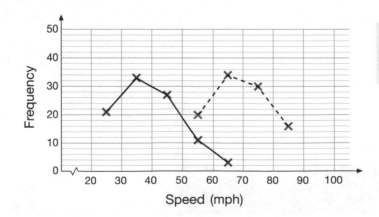

Key:
——— B1026
------- M1

The diagrams show that the two distributions have similar shapes but the speeds of the motorway are about 30 mph higher on average.

Top Tip!

If you are asked to compare distributions, comment on the shape, the spread (if it is significantly different) and the average values. The average will be in about the middle of the distribution.

Stem-and-leaf diagrams

- A **stem-and-leaf diagram** shows **ordered** data in a **concise** way.

Example: Show the data 32, 41, 56, 37, 38, 29, 42, 46, 38, 28, 34, 38, 37, 51, 49 on a stem-and-leaf diagram.

The **stem** is the **10s digit** and the **leaves** are the **units**.

2	8	9					
3	2	4	7	7	8	8	8
4	1	2	6	9			
5	1	6					

Key: 2 | 8 represents 28

Top Tip!
Always put a **key** on a stem-and-leaf diagram.

Sample worked test question

The frequency diagram shows the number of lengths 20 students swam in a sponsored swim.

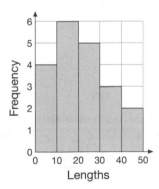

a How many students swam more than 20 lengths?

b The teacher wants to know the greatest number of lengths that anyone swam.

Tick the correct box:

☐ 50   ☐ 40   ☐ 45   ☐ Cannot tell

Explain your answer.

Answers

a *5 students swam between 20 and 30 lengths, 3 swam between 30 and 40 lengths and 2 swam between 40 and 50 lengths. This is a total of 10 students.*

b *Cannot tell. All you know is that 3 students swam between 40 and 50 lengths, not how many lengths they swam.*

Did You Know?
A Blue Whale's belly button is about 8 inches wide.

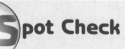**pot Check**

1 Put the following data under the correct headings in the table: height of boys aged 15; marks in a spelling test out of 10; makes of cars; number of matches in 10 boxes; time taken to run 100 metres.

Discrete data	Continuous data

HANDLING DATA — Scatter diagrams

Scatter diagrams

- A **scatter diagram** shows the relationship between two variables, for example: the temperature and the sales of ice cream.

- The mathematical name for the relationship is **correlation**.

  The following diagrams show the different types of correlation.

Strong, positive correlation

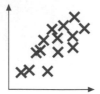

Weak, positive correlation

No correlation

Weak, negative correlation

Strong, negative correlation

Example: The scatter on the right diagram shows the relationship between the cost of taxi fares and distances of journeys.

a Describe the correlation between the variables.

b Describe the expected correlation between the following:

　i The cost of a taxi journey and the age of the taxi driver.

　ii The time of a taxi journey and the number of cars on the road.

　iii The distance of a taxi journey and the time of the journey.

a The diagram shows weak, positive correlation.

b i There will be no correlation between the age of a driver and the cost of a journey.

　ii The time of a taxi journey will increase with more cars on the road, so it would show weak, positive correlation.

　iii The longer a journey, the more time it would take so there is positive correlation.

Line of best fit

- A **line of best fit** is a line that passes through the data and passes as close to as many of the points as possible. It can be used to predict values.

Example: This scatter diagram shows the top speed and engine size of some cars, and a line of best fit.

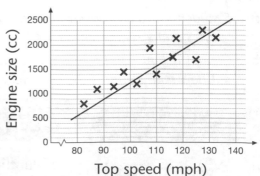

a What does the scatter diagram show about the relationship between the engine size and top speed of cars?

b The top speed of a car is 120 mph. Use the line of best fit to estimate the engine size.

a The scatter diagram shows that cars with a larger engine have a higher top speed.

b Going up from 120 mph on the Top speed axis to the line of best fit and across to the Engine size axis gives 1900 cc.

Sample mental test question

Describe the correlation in the diagram.

The correlation is weak negative but you would still get marks for writing 'negative correlation'.

Sample worked test question

A fish breeder keeps records of the age and mass of his prize carp. He plots the results on a scatter diagram.

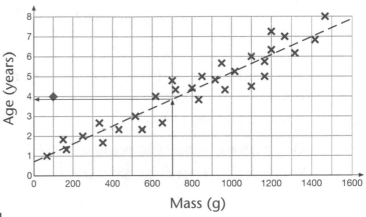

a   A fish is 4 years old and weighs 100 g.
Explain why this fish is not likely to be a carp.

b   The breeder is given a carp that weighs 700 g but he does not know how old it is.
He only uses fish for breeding if they are over 5 years old. Will this fish be suitable for breeding?
Give a reason for your answer.

Answers

a   *The data shows strong positive correlation.*
Plot the point (100, 4). (This is shown as a diamond.)
It is clear that this point is well away from the others. It does not have the same correlation as the other values so the fish is unlikely to be a carp.

b   *Draw the line of best fit. (This is shown dashed.)*
Draw a line from 700 g up to the line of best fit and then across to the Age axis. (These are the solid lines.)
This comes to just under 4 years.
Therefore the fish may not be old enough for breeding.

Did You Know?

A human can jump about four times their body length. A flea can jump 350 times its body length.

Spot Check

1 Describe the expected correlation between:
   a   the temperature and the number of cold drinks sold
   b   the time of a journey and the average speed.

Surveys

- **Surveys** are used to find out information. Groups, such as the government, need information so they can plan for the future. Companies need to know who buys their products.

- Information is usually collected using a **questionnaire**.

- For example, if you want to find out if students would like to have a party, you would want to know what day they would prefer, what type of refreshments, what type of music and how much they would pay.

- Questions in a questionnaire should be **unbiased**.

Example: This is a question on a survey about which day to hold a party.

> You would prefer a party on Friday, wouldn't you?
> Yes ☐   No ☐

This question is biased as it forces an opinion on the person being surveyed.

A better question would be:

> On which day would you prefer a party?
> Thursday ☐   Friday ☐   Saturday ☐

Top Tip!
Don't ask personal questions such as 'How old are you?' and expect an answer. People may be embarrassed to give their age.

Response sections

- Questions should have a simple response section with clear choices, no overlapping responses and a wide range of responses.

Example: Look at this question from a survey with a response section.

> How old are you?
> Under 10 ☐   10–20 ☐   20–30 ☐   Over 30 ☐

The response section of this question has overlapping categories.

A better question would be:

> How old are you?
> Under 10 ☐   11–20 ☐   21–30 ☐   31 or over ☐

Top Tip!
Keep questions short and with a small choice of answers. Make your responses simple so you can use tick boxes.

Sampling

- You also need to be very careful about where you undertake a survey and who you ask.

  If the school has a Friday lunchtime party and you did your survey there, you would get a **biased sample** as the students are likely to say 'yes'.

  If you just asked a Year 7 tutor group, they might not want a party and the views of the Year 11s would not have been taken into account. This would be a **non-representative sample**.

- You should make sure the people who are surveyed are from a range of age groups and have **different views**.

Top Tip!

One way to ensure an unbiased and representative sample is to choose the people you survey **randomly**. For example, you could put all the names in a hat and draw some out. In a **random sample** everyone has an **equal chance** of being picked for the sample.

Sample worked test question

Year 9 are planning a trip and some students decide to do a survey about where people want to go.

a This is one of Ricky's questions.

> Do you want to go paintballing?
>
> Yes ☐ No ☐

What is wrong with this question?

b This is another question.

> How much are you willing to spend?
>
> £0–£10 ☐   £0–£15 ☐   Over £20 ☐

What is wrong with this question?

c Ricky decides to ask all the boys in his football practice group. What is wrong with this method of doing the survey?

Answers

a   *There are not enough choices. Ricky is probably trying to get everyone to agree to go paintballing.*

b   *The responses overlap so someone wanting to spend £9 would have two boxes to tick.*

c   *They will all have similar opinions. The sample is non-representative and will give a biased response.*

Did You Know?

The first public opinion surveys started in 1935 and the first question ever asked was: 'Do you think expenditures by the government for relief and recovery are too little, too great, or just about right?'. You could find several things wrong with this question!

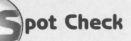

Spot Check

1 Give two reasons why this is not a good question in a survey: 'Fast food makes you fat and is unhealthy. Do you agree?'

Yes ☐   No ☐

The probability scale

- **Probability** is the **chance** that something will happen.
- An event that is **impossible** has a probability of 0.
  An event that is **certain** has a probability of 1.
  All other probabilities are between 0 and 1.
- The probability scale runs from 0 to 1.
- Various words can be used to describe probability such as:
  impossible, very unlikely, unlikely, evens, likely, very likely and certain.
  On a probability scale these would be:

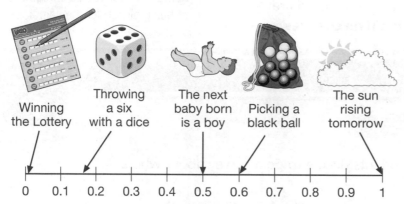

Winning the Lottery   Throwing a six with a dice   The next baby born is a boy   Picking a black ball   The sun rising tomorrow

0 0.1 0.2 0.3 0.4 0.5 0.6 0.7 0.8 0.9 1

Example: A bag contains 7 blue balls and 1 red ball.

a Imat is going to take a ball at random from the bag.

He says, 'There are two colours so it is equally likely that I will take a blue ball as a red ball'.

Explain why Imat is wrong.

b Complete the following sentences using the words below:

| impossible   very unlikely   unlikely   evens   likely   very likely   certain |

A ball is taken at random from the bag.
The probability of taking a blue ball is ……………………………… .
The probability of taking a green ball is ……………………………… .

c How many red balls must be put in the bag to make the chance of taking a red ball evens?

a There are unequal numbers of each colour in the bag.
The probability of blue is $\frac{7}{8}$ and red is $\frac{1}{8}$.

b The probability of getting a blue ball is **very likely**.
The probability of getting a green ball is **impossible**.

c To make the probability evens, there should be the same number of each colour.
So 6 red balls need to be added.

Probability of events

- The total probability of all possible events is 1.
- These are examples of **mutually exclusive** events:

  P(boy) + P(girl) = 1

  P(head) + P(tail) = 1.

  The probability of an event is P(event) = $\dfrac{\text{number of ways event can happen}}{\text{number of total outcomes}}$

Example: **a** If the chance of picking a black ball from the bag shown here is $\frac{6}{10}$ or $\frac{3}{5}$, what is the chance of picking a white ball?

a You can see that there are four white balls so the chance of picking a white ball is $\frac{4}{10}$ or $\frac{2}{5}$.

Note that $\frac{6}{10} + \frac{4}{10} = 1$ and $\frac{3}{5} + \frac{2}{5} = 1$

Top Tip!

Unless the question asks for an answer in 'its simplest form', you do not have to cancel fractions, but be careful if you do.

Top Tip!

You need to add up the total number of balls to find the denominator of the fraction.

Sample worked test question

A box of juice drinks contains four orange, three grapefruit, two cranberry and one lemon drink. A drink is taken at random from the box.

a What is the probability it is orange?

b What is the probability that it is not lemon?

c Priti drinks two orange juices. She then takes a drink at random from the remaining drinks. What is the probability she takes a cranberry juice?

Answers

a *P(orange)* = $\frac{4}{10}$ = $\frac{2}{5}$

b *P(not lemon)* = $\frac{9}{10}$

c *There are only 8 drinks left, 2 are cranberry.*

  P(cranberry) = $\frac{2}{8}$ = $\frac{1}{4}$

Top Tip!

There are 9 out of 10 that are not lemon but it can also be worked out as

1 − P(lemon)

$1 - \frac{1}{10} = \frac{9}{10}$

Did You Know?

The probability of winning the lottery is 1 in 14 million.

Spot Check

1 A bag contains 4 red counters and 8 blue counters. A counter is taken out at random.

What is the probability that the counter is: **a** red **b** blue **c** green?

Probability

- The probability of an event is the number of ways that event can happen divided by the total number of outcomes.

  Consider throwing a two on a dice. There is one way of throwing a two, and six ways the dice can land, so P(2 with a dice) = $\frac{1}{6}$.

Example: When a dice is thrown, what is the probability of:

a a score of 4   **b** a square number   **c** a factor of 24?

The dice can land six ways.

a There is only one 4 so P(4) = $\frac{1}{6}$

b Square numbers are 1 and 4, so P(square) = $\frac{2}{6}$ = $\frac{1}{3}$

c The factors of 24 on a dice are 1, 2, 3, 4, 6 so
   P(factors of 24) = $\frac{5}{6}$

Example: A box contains 21 copper nails and 9 steel nails.

A nail is taken out at random.

a What is the probability that it is a copper nail?
   Give your answer as a fraction in its simplest form.

b Give your answer to part **a** as a percentage.

c The first nail is put back in the box. Then six nails are taken out of the box.

   After the nails are removed, the probability of taking a copper nail at random is $\frac{7}{8}$.

   Explain how you know that the six nails taken out were steel nails.

a P(copper) = $\frac{21}{30}$ = $\frac{7}{10}$

b $\frac{7}{10}$ = 70%

c There are now 24 nails in the box.
   If P(copper) = $\frac{7}{8}$ = $\frac{21}{24}$, then there are still 21 copper nails in the box.
   So the nails removed must have been steel nails.

Top Tip!

You need to know the equivalent decimals and percentages for some simple fractions.

Spot Check

1 A bag contains 6 red, 4 blue and 10 green balls. A ball is taken out at random.

   What is the probability that the ball is:
   a red   **b** green   **c** not blue?

2 The word 'statistics' is spelled out on cards.

   The cards are shuffled and one is chosen at random.
   What is the probability that:

   a it is the letter I

   b it is an S or a T

   c it is one of the letters in the word CAST?

Combined events

- Sometimes two separate events can take place at the same time; for example, throwing a dice and tossing a coin.
- The mathematical name for events like this is **independent**, because the outcome of throwing the dice does not have any influence on the outcome of tossing the coin.
- The combined outcomes of the two events can be shown in different ways.
- They can be written as a **list**:

  (1, head), (1, tail), (2, head), (2, tail), (3, head), (3, tail),

  (4, head), (4, tail), (5, head), (5, tail), (6, head), (6, tail)

- They can also be shown in a **sample space** diagram:

- You can see that there are 12 outcomes for the **combined events**.

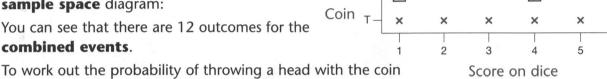

  Coin

  Score on dice

  To work out the probability of throwing a head with the coin and a square number on the dice, you would need to count which of the 12 outcomes satisfy the conditions.

  These are shown in a box on the sample space diagram. So P(head and square number) = $\frac{2}{12} = \frac{1}{6}$

Sample mental test question

A box of toffee contains hard and soft toffees only. The probability of taking a hard toffee is $\frac{8}{15}$.
What is the probability of taking a soft toffee?

The probability of a hard toffee is $\frac{8}{15}$, so the probability of a soft toffee is $1 - \frac{8}{15} = \frac{7}{15}$.

Sample worked test question

Two four-sided dice numbered from 1 to 4 are thrown together.
The scores are multiplied together.

a Complete the sample space diagram showing the possible scores of the combined event.

b Find the probability that the combined score is:

  i an even number   **ii** a square number   **iii** a factor of 144.

Score on second dice

	1	2	3	4
1	1	2		
2			6	
3		6	9	
4	4	8	12	16

Score on first dice

Answers

a

Score on second dice

	1	2	3	4
1	1	2	3	4
2	2	4	6	8
3	3	6	9	12
4	4	8	12	16

Score on first dice

b i *There are 16 outcomes and 12 of them are even numbers.* $P(even) = \frac{12}{16} = \frac{3}{4}$

ii *There are 6 square numbers: 1, 4, 4, 4, 9, 16.* $P(square) = \frac{6}{16} = \frac{3}{8}$

iii *All of the numbers are factors of 144.* $P(factor\ of\ 144) = 1$

Did You Know?

If you are in a room with 30 strangers, the chance that one of them has the same birthday as you is over a half.

Index

Answers to Spot Check questions

p. 5   **1** 1.02, 1.2, 1.3, 1.324
       2 a 6543   **b** 634 or 654   **c** 5.3 or 5.4   **d** 3.6

p. 6   **1 a** 656   **b** 9090   **c** 574   **d** 536   **e** 52
       f 176 remainder 4

p. 8   **1** 0.645, 1.89, 2.3   **b** 2.3   **c** 3.4

p. 10   **1** 1924   **2** 54

p. 12   **1 a** 6000   **b** 6

p. 15   **1 a** 70   **b** 0.452   **c** 18.72   **d** 1.47

p. 16   **1 a** −9   **b** +9   **c** +12   **d** −5

p. 19   **1 a** $\frac{5}{6}$ **b** $\frac{6}{7}$
       2 a $\frac{17}{20}$ **b** $\frac{7}{12}$

p. 21   **1 a** $\frac{1}{6}$ **b** 3
       2 a $\frac{5}{12}$ **b** $1\frac{1}{3}$

p. 23   **1**

Decimal	Percentage	Fraction
0.15	15%	$\frac{3}{20}$
0.35	35%	$\frac{7}{20}$
0.9	90%	$\frac{9}{10}$

p. 25   **1 a** £90   **b** 105.6 kg

p. 26   **1** 7 : 9
       2 £12 : £20

p. 29   **1** 23   **2** 4*n*   **3** 4*n* + 1

p. 31   **a** 9   **b** 3   **c** 12   **d** 21

p. 33   **1 a** 2*a* + 4   **b** 20*b*²
       2 a 32   **b** 25

p. 35   **1** 7
       2 6

p. 37   **1** (5, −2)
       2 *x*-axis

p. 39   **1**

x	−2	−1	0	1	2	3	4
y	−8	−5	−2	1	4	7	10

p. 41   **1** A is *x* = 2, B is *x* + *y* = 5, C is *y* = 4

p. 43   **1 a** 7.5   **b** 10
       2 (9 + 6) ÷ 3 + 5 = 10

p. 45   **1 a** *x* = 6   **b** *x* = 10
       2 a 6.5   **b** −1   **c** 0   **d** −0.25

p. 47   **1 a** *x* = 13   **b** *x* = −6
       2 a 4.5   **b** 3   **c** Because 3*x* + 7 = 3*x* + 1 means 7 = 1.

p. 49   **1** 2 × (3)³ + 3 × 3 = 63, 2 × (4)³ + 3 × 4 = 140

p. 51   **1** 7 hours and 35 minutes
       2 2 hours and 35 minutes

p. 53   **1 a** mm   **b** cl or ml   **c** km
       2 a 340 cm   **b** 4.5 l   **c** 5000 kg   **d** 9.8 cm

p. 55   **1** No, 20 kg is about 45 lb
       2 a 68 inches   **b** 1 m 70 cm

p. 57   **1 a** obtuse angle = between 90° and 180°   **b** reflex
       angle = between 180° and 360°
       2 a 090°   **b** 180°   **c** 270°

p. 59   **1** *x* = 72°
       2 *a* = 70°, *b* = 79°

p. 61   **1** *a* = 120°, *b* = 60°
       2 *a* = 61°, *b* = 88°, c = 51°

p. 62   **1 a** 3   **b** 3
       2 a 2   **b** 4   **c** 1

p. 64   **1**

p. 67   **1**

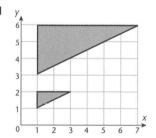

       2 Scale factor 2, centre (0, 4)

p. 68   **1** A and C

p. 70   **1** Perimeter 24 cm, area 28 cm²

p. 73   **1** Circumference 31.4 cm, area 78.5 cm²
       2 21.98 m²

p. 75   **1** Volume 24 cm³, surface area 52 cm²

p. 77   **1** Mode 1, range 3

p. 78   **1** Mode 24, median 23, mean 22

p. 81   **1 a** mean 7, range 6   **b** mean 7, range 11

p. 83   **1 a** about 5 °C   **b** It's not possible to estimate as
       the temperature may not continue to decrease at
       same rate.
       2 Between 3 and 4 as the graph is the steepest.

p. 85   **1** 84°
       2 a If there were 30 students, each student would be
       represented by 12° and 20° is not a multiple of 12.
       b There could be 18 students, or any multiple of 18.
       36 is the most likely number.

p. 87   **1**

Discrete data	Continuous data
marks in spelling test	height of boys
makes of cars	time to run 100 m
number of matches	

p. 89   **1 a** (Weak) positive correlation   **b** (strong) negative
       correlation

p. 91   **1** Leading (or offensive) question. Not enough
       response sections.

p. 93   **1 a** $\frac{4}{12} = \frac{1}{3}$ **b** $\frac{8}{12} = \frac{2}{3}$ **c** 0

p. 94   **1 a** $\frac{6}{20} = \frac{3}{10}$ **b** $\frac{10}{20} = \frac{1}{2}$ **c** $\frac{16}{20} = \frac{4}{5}$
       2 a $\frac{1}{5}$ **b** $\frac{3}{5}$ **c** $\frac{4}{5}$

Collins

Collins Revision

KS3

Maths

Workbook

Levels 3-6

Keith Gordon

1 Four friends finish a game of Scrabble®.

I scored one
hundred and six

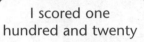

I scored
eighty-nine

I scored one
hundred and twenty

I scored
ninety- three

Olivia

Daniel

Emily

Jerzy

a Who won the game?

_____

1 mark

b Write the scores in figures, starting with the largest.

_____ , _____ , _____ , _____

2 marks

2 a What number is 100 less than 399?

_____

1 mark

b What number is 1 less than 3.1?

_____

1 mark

3 Here are 5 number cards. | 6 | 9 | 4 | 5 | 1 |

Jade picks three cards and makes this number. | 4 | 9 | 5 |

Carlos picks three cards and makes this number. | 6 | 1 | 5 |

a Make a larger number than 495 with Jade's three cards.

_____

1 mark

b Make a smaller odd number than 615 with Carlos' three cards.

_____

1 mark

c Using any three of the cards make an even number between 495 and 615.

_____

1 mark

4 The attendance at a football game was 8007.

   a Write the number 8007 in words.

_____

   b The capacity of the ground is 10 000. How many more fans could have attended?

_____

5 Write down the value of the number halfway between the numbers shown

   a

15   [ ]   23

   b

1.1   [ ]   1.4

6 A three-digit number is made from three number cards 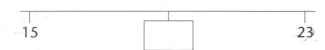   3   7   2

   when the digits are reversed the number becomes   2   7   3

   a What is the difference between 372 and 273?

_____

   b Which digit represents the same value in each number?

_____

7 Fill in the missing numbers on the number line.

| 6.6 | 6.7 | | | | |

levels
3-4

1 Write in the missing numbers.

a | 37 | + | 26 | = | [ ]

1 mark

b | 37 | – | [ ] | = | 16 |

1 mark

2 Find the answer to the following.

a 634 + 179

_____

1 mark

b 518 – 329

_____

1 mark

3 Work out the following.

a Add 178 to half of 248.

_____

2 marks

b Add 145 to 325, then subtract 275.

_____

2 marks

4 Fill in the missing numbers.

a 514 + _____ = 677   **b** 873 – _____ = 576

c _____ – 226 = 514   **d** _____ + 371 = 482

4 marks

5 Each side of the triangle adds up to the same number.
Use these numbers to complete the triangle.

(2) (3) (6)

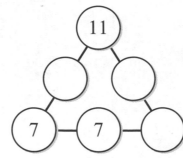

2 marks

6 a Salma did a sponsored swim.
She swam 9 lengths and collected
35 pence for every length.
How much did she collect altogether?
Give your answer in pounds.

_____

 1 mark

b Ingrid also did a sponsored swim.
She was sponsored 80p per length and raised a total of £19.20.
How many lengths did she swim?

_____

 1 mark

7 Fill in the missing numbers.

a 46 x _____ = 828   **b** 684 ÷ _____ = 36

c _____ x 22 = 748   **d** _____ ÷ 37 = 15

4 marks

8 A lottery syndicate wins £225 000.
a There are 25 members in the syndicate who get an equal share of the winnings.

How much does each member of the syndicate receive?

_____

 1 mark

b Ben, one of the members, decides to share £4500 of his winnings between
his 9 grandchildren. How much does each child receive?

_____

 1 mark

9 There are 8 pencils in a box. A box of pencils costs £1.44.
a How many pencils are there in 15 boxes?

_____

 1 mark

b How much does each pencil cost?

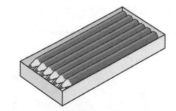

_____

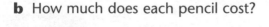 **1 mark**

1 Work out the following.

   a 0.4 + 0.7 _____

   1 mark

   b 2.7 – 1.3 _____

   1 mark

   c 3.2 + 4.97 _____

   1 mark

   d 36.34 – 16.5 _____

   1 mark

2 **a** Johannes pays £1.25 for a bus ticket to work and £1.10 for a bus ticket on the way home from work.
How much does he pay altogether?

   _____

   1 mark

   b How much would he save if he bought a day pass for £1.80?

   _____

   1 mark

3 Here are 5 cards.   3   0   .   8   5

   a Make a number between 3 and 4 with three of the cards. ☐ ☐ ☐

   1 mark

   b Make a number less than 0.5 with three of the cards. ☐ ☐ ☐

   1 mark

4 Put the following decimals in order with the smallest first.

   1.23,   3.21,   2.3,   0.1

   _____ , _____ , _____ , _____

   1 mark

5 a Adam buys a burger, fries and a drink.
How much does he pay?

£1.85   95p   65p

_____

b A 'Meal Deal' gives a burger, fries and a drink for £2.95.
How much would Adam save with a 'Meal Deal'?

_____

1 mark

6 The map shows three towns A, B and C and the distances between them.

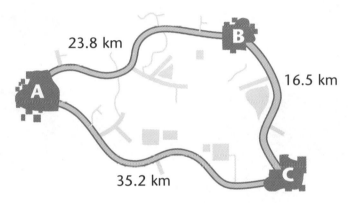

23.8 km

16.5 km

35.2 km

a Cameron drives from A to B and then to C.

How far does he travel altogether? _____

 1 mark

b How much further does he travel than the direct route from A to C?

_____

 1 mark

7 Put the signs < (less than), > (greater than) or = (equals) between these statements to make them true. The first is done for you.

a 2.3 + 1.7 > 6.5 – 3.1

b 3.5 – 0.8 _____ 2.6 + 0.2

c 1.98 + 3.1 _____ 2.98 + 2.1

d 6 – 4.7 _____ 2 + 0.3

3 marks

8 Write a number to complete these calculations. The first is done for you.

a 6.2 + 0.8 = 4.2 + 2.8

b 5.6 ~~−~~ 2.8 = 7.6 – _____
(2.8 written above)

c 1.2 + 6.7 = 5.2 + _____

d 8 – 1.6 = 7 – _____

3 marks

NUMBER

Long multiplication and division

level 5

1 Work out the following.

   a 27 x 32

<u>   </u> **2 marks**

   b 36 x 217

<u>   </u> **2 marks**

   c 952 ÷ 28

<u>   </u> **2 marks**

   d 994 ÷ 14

<u>   </u> **2 marks**

2 **a** Eggs are delivered in trays of 48.
How many eggs will be in 17 trays?

<u>   </u> **2 marks**

   b A restaurant orders 1000 eggs.

     i How many full trays will they need? <u>   </u> **2 marks**

     ii How many eggs will be in the last tray? <u>   </u> **2 marks**

3 One bus carries 52 passengers.

   a How many passengers could be
carried on 23 buses?

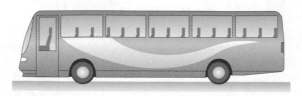

<u>   </u> **2 marks**

   b A school is taking 950 students to a theme park at the end of term.
How many buses will they need to hire?

<u>   </u> **2 marks**

4 Maths textbooks are sold in packs of 15.

   a A school orders 24 packs.

     How many books are there in 24 packs?

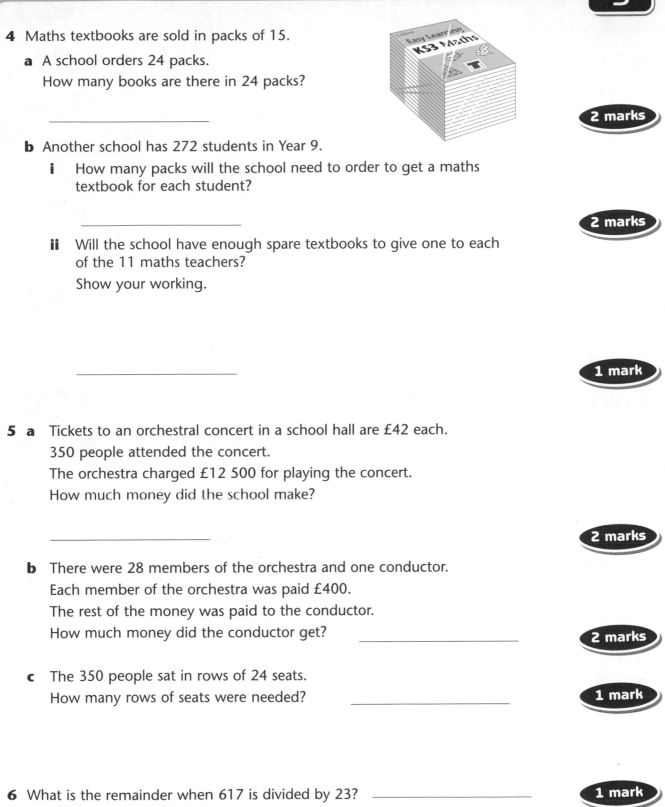

_____

   b Another school has 272 students in Year 9.

     i How many packs will the school need to order to get a maths textbook for each student?

_____

2 marks

     ii Will the school have enough spare textbooks to give one to each of the 11 maths teachers?

      Show your working.

_____

1 mark

5 **a** Tickets to an orchestral concert in a school hall are £42 each.

    350 people attended the concert.

    The orchestra charged £12 500 for playing the concert.

    How much money did the school make?

_____

2 marks

   b There were 28 members of the orchestra and one conductor.

    Each member of the orchestra was paid £400.

    The rest of the money was paid to the conductor.

    How much money did the conductor get? _____

2 marks

   c The 350 people sat in rows of 24 seats.

    How many rows of seats were needed? _____

1 mark

6 What is the remainder when 617 is divided by 23? _____

1 mark

7 How many boxes of cakes, each holding 12 cakes, will be needed to give 120 guests at a garden party three cakes each?

1 mark

_____

Rounding and approximation

levels 3-4

1 Round off the number 367 to

a the nearest 10 ______________________ 1 mark

b the nearest 100 ______________________ 1 mark

2 Round off the number 4562 to

a the nearest 10 ______________________ 1 mark

b the nearest 100 ______________________ 1 mark

c the nearest 1000 ______________________ 1 mark

3 Round off the number 5.687 to

a 1 decimal place ______________________ 1 mark

b 2 decimal places ______________________ 1 mark

4 Round off the following numbers to 1 significant figure.

a 2762 ______________________ 1 mark

b 5.92 ______________________ 1 mark

c 183 ______________________ 1 mark

d 0.079 ______________________ 1 mark

5 The picture shows a man standing by a bus.

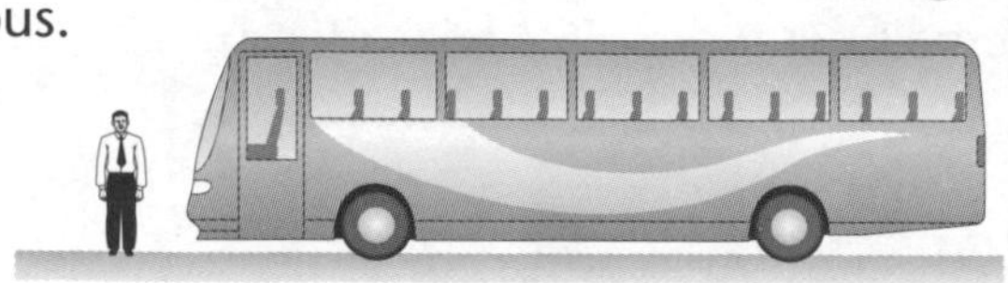

a Estimate the height of the bus.

______________________ 1 mark

b Estimate the length of the bus.

______________________ 1 mark

6 By rounding these numbers to 1 significant figure, estimate answers
to these calculations.

   a 49.6 x 11.3 _____

 2 marks

   b 187 ÷ 38.6 _____

2 marks

7 By rounding these numbers to 1 significant figure, estimate answers
to these calculations.

   a $\dfrac{198 + 421}{23 + 12}$ _____

1 mark

   b $\dfrac{32.7 \times 59.8}{19.3}$ _____

1 mark

8 A jar of sweets is labelled 'Contains 100 sweets (to the nearest 10)'.

   a What is the least number of sweets in the jar? _____

 1 mark

   b What is the greatest possible number of sweets in the jar?

   _____

 1 mark

9 Class 9R are making Christmas cards.
The cards are 6 cm by 8 cm, each side being
measured to the nearest cm.
Envelopes are made to a size of 9 cm by 7 cm.

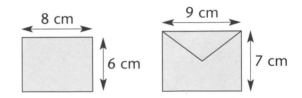

   a Explain why cards cannot be any wider than $8\frac{1}{2}$ cm.

   _____

1 mark

   b What is the smallest height the envelopes could be?

   _____

 1 mark

   c Explain why the cards will fit into the envelopes.

   _____

 1 mark

NUMBER

Multiplying and dividing decimals

1 Look at these five cards.  | 2 | 5 | 6 | . | 0 |

    a Deepak picks two cards and makes the number 25.

    Which extra card should he pick to make his number 10 times bigger?

    _____

     1 mark

    b Samuel picks three cards and makes the number 5.6

    Show the three cards Samuel needs to make a number that is
100 times bigger than 5.6

     1 mark

2 The diagram shows how to change metres into millimetres.

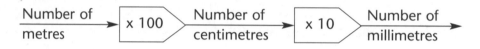

Number of metres → ×100 → Number of centimetres → ×10 → Number of millimetres

    a Change 3.4 metres into millimetres.

    _____

     1 mark

    b Change 74 millimetres into metres.

    _____

     1 mark

3 Fill in the missing numbers.

    a $5 \div 10 =$ _____   **b** _____ $\times 100 = 23$

    c $0.6 \div 100 =$ _____   **d** $0.6 \times$ _____ $= 60$

     4 marks

4 Paul spends £17.10 each week on train fares.

    a How much would he spend on train fares on 4 weeks?

    _____

     1 mark

    b How much would he save with a monthly pass that costs £56.50?

     1 mark

5 Complete this tuck shop order.

100 Mars bars at £0.37 each   £ _____

100 Twix bars at £0.35 each   £ _____

50 Mini fudge bars at £0.18 each   £ _____

                        Total   £ _____

4 marks

6 Maria bought 3 CDs and 5 DVDs.

How much does she pay altogether?

£15.95

£8.99

_____

2 marks

7 Jamal buys 5 new tyres for his car.
The total bill is £325.
How much was each tyre?

_____

1 mark

8 Work out the following.

a 4.6 x 7 = _____   **b** 35.4 ÷ 6 = _____

c 8 x 5.2 = _____   **d** 58.1 ÷ 7 = _____

4 marks

9 Six people buy a meal in a restaurant and
the bill comes to £256.80.

If they share the cost equally how much
does each person pay?

_____

1 mark

NUMBER — Negative numbers

1 The number line shows the surface temperature of the planets.

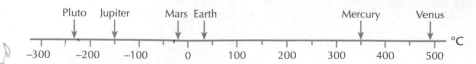

Pluto Jupiter Mars Earth Mercury Venus

-300 -200 -100 0 100 200 300 400 500 °C

a Which planet has a temperature of about –20 °C?

_____

 1 mark

b Which planet has a temperature of about 350 °C?

_____

1 mark

c What is the approximate difference in temperature between the coldest and the warmest planet?

_____

1 mark

2 Look at this list of numbers.

–7, –6, –2, –1, 0, 2, 4, 8

a What is the total of all eight numbers?

_____

1 mark

b Choose three different numbers that have the lowest total.

_____

1 mark

c Choose two numbers so that the product is as low as possible.

_____

1 mark

3 The diagram shows how to change °C into °F.

Temperature (°C) → ÷ 5 → x 9 → + 32 → Temperature (°F)

a Change 20 °C into °F. _____

1 mark

b Change –40 °C into °F. _____

1 mark

c Change –4 °F into °C. _____

1 mark

4 Using = (equals), < (less than) or > (greater than), put the correct sign between each number sentence. The first one has been done for you.

a 5 − 6 < 6 − 5

b −9 _____ −3

c +7 − −8 _____ +8 − −7

d 4 x −2 _____ −4 x 2

3 marks

5 Work out the following.

a −8 + 3 − 6 _____

b −3 x −2 + 5 _____

c −32 ÷ + 8 _____

d (−4 − 3) x −6 _____

4 marks

6 Fill in two **negative** numbers to make the following true.

a ☐ + ☐ = −5

2 marks

b ☐ − ☐ = −5

2 marks

7 Write the missing numbers on the number lines.

a

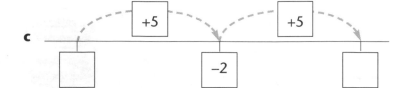

+27

☐   13

b

☐

−15   −8

c

+5   +5

☐   −2   ☐

4 marks

NUMBER

Adding and subtracting fractions

1 The table shows some fractions of amounts of money.

	£8	£10	£22
$\frac{1}{2}$	£4.00	£5.00	£11.00
$\frac{1}{4}$	£2.00	£2.50	£5.50
$\frac{1}{8}$	£1.00	£1.25	£2.75

Use the table to work out the missing numbers.

a $\frac{3}{8}$ of £22 = _____

b £7.50 = _____ of £10

c £5 = $\frac{5}{8}$ of _____

d £4 = $\frac{1}{8}$ of _____

4 marks

2 Work out the missing numbers or fractions.

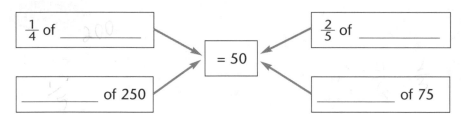

$\frac{1}{4}$ of _____

_____ of 250

= 50

$\frac{2}{5}$ of _____

_____ of 75

4 marks

3 Work out the missing numbers.

a $\frac{4}{12} = \frac{\square}{3}$

b $\frac{5}{7} = \frac{15}{\square}$

2 marks

4 a How many sixths are there in $2\frac{5}{6}$? _____

1 mark

b How many sixths are in $1\frac{2}{3}$? _____

1 mark

5 Work out the following.

a $\frac{1}{3} + \frac{2}{5}$ _____ **2 marks**

b $\frac{3}{5} - \frac{1}{4}$ _____ **2 marks**

6 Work out the following.

a $2\frac{1}{4} + 3\frac{1}{5}$ _____ **2 marks**

b $2\frac{3}{4} - 1\frac{1}{3}$ _____ **2 marks**

7 The diagram shows a grey rectangle that is 8 cm by 6 cm. Two black squares, one 4 cm by 4 cm and the other 2 cm by 2 cm, are drawn inside it.

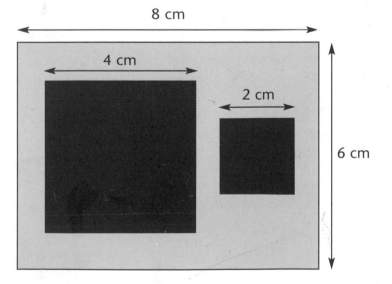

a What fraction of the rectangle is shaded black?

_____ **2 marks**

b What fraction of the rectangle is shaded grey?

_____ **2 marks**

NUMBER

Multiplying and dividing fractions

1 What is the highest common factor of 12 and 42?
Tick the correct answer.

☐ 12   ☐ 42   ☐ 2   ☑ 6

1 mark

2 What is the mixed number $3\frac{2}{3}$, when written as a top-heavy fraction?
Tick the correct answer.

☐ $\frac{32}{3}$ ☑ $\frac{11}{3}$ ☐ $\frac{12}{3}$ ☐ 0.66

1 mark

3 The fraction of red balls placed in a bag is $\frac{1}{3}$. Half of these red balls are taken out.
What fraction of the red balls is in the bag now?
Tick the correct answer.

☐ $\frac{1}{3}$ ☐ $\frac{1}{5}$ ☐ $\frac{1}{6}$ ☐ $\frac{1}{12}$

1 mark

4 Some examples of multiplying fractions are shown.

$\frac{2}{3} \times \frac{4}{5} = \frac{8}{15}$, $\frac{1}{4} \times \frac{3}{7} = \frac{3}{28}$, $\frac{3}{5} \times \frac{4}{11} = \frac{12}{55}$

Which of the following is the answer to $\frac{a}{b} \times \frac{c}{d}$?
Tick the correct answer.

☐ $\frac{a}{cbd}$ ☐ $\frac{ac}{bd}$ ☐ $\frac{ad}{cb}$ ☐ $\frac{ab}{cd}$

1 mark

5 What is $\frac{3}{4} \times \frac{1}{6}$ in its simplest form? _____

1 mark

6 Work out $\frac{1}{8} \div \frac{5}{6}$ and give the answer in its simplest form.

_____

1 mark

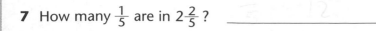
7 How many $\frac{1}{5}$ are in $2\frac{2}{5}$? _____

8 The table shows some fractions of different weights.

	7.5 kg	12 kg	21 kg
$\frac{1}{2}$	3.75 kg	6 kg	10.5 kg
$\frac{1}{3}$	2.5 kg	4 kg	7 kg
$\frac{1}{6}$	1.25 kg	2 kg	3.5 kg

Use the table to work out the missing numbers.

a $\frac{2}{3}$ x 28.5 kg = _____

b 5.5 kg = _____ x 33 kg

c 6.5 kg = $\frac{1}{3}$ x _____

d 6.75 kg = $\frac{1}{6}$ x _____

 4 marks

9 Work out the following.

a $\frac{1}{9}$ x $\frac{3}{5}$

_____ 1 mark

b $\frac{3}{10}$ ÷ $\frac{6}{25}$

_____ 1 mark

10 Work out the following.

a $2\frac{1}{4}$ x $1\frac{1}{5}$

_____ 2 marks

b $2\frac{3}{4}$ ÷ $4\frac{1}{8}$

_____   2 marks

NUMBER

Equivalent fractions, percentages and decimals

1 Fill in the equivalent fractions, percentages and decimals as appropriate. The first line has been done for you.

	Fraction	Percentage	Decimal
a	$\frac{1}{4}$	25%	0.25
b	$\frac{3}{5}$		
c		75%	
d			0.9

6 marks

2 a Complete these sentences.

  i _____ **out of 10** is the same as 60%.

1 mark

  ii **24 out of 50** is the same as _____ %.

1 mark

  b Complete these sentences using different pairs of numbers.

  i _____ out of _____ is the same as 20%.

1 mark

  ii _____ out of _____ is the same as 20%.

1 mark

3 About 40% of this shape is shaded grey.

  a Approximately what percentage is striped? _____

1 mark

  b Approximately what percentage is white? _____

1 mark

4 Look at the diagram.

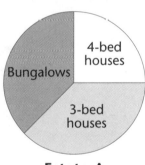

a   What fraction is shaded? _____

b   What percentage is shaded? _____

5 The pie charts show the types of houses in two housing estates.

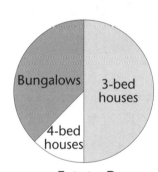

Estate A   Estate B

a   What percentage of the houses on estate A are 4-bed houses? _____

b   What fraction of the houses on estate B are bungalows? _____

c   Tick the statement that is true.

☐   There are more bungalows on estate A than B.

☐   There are fewer bungalows on estate A than B.

☐   There are equal numbers of bungalows on estate A and B.

☐   You cannot tell how many bungalows are on each estate.

1 Alex asked 50 children what their favourite lunch was.

Lunch	Boys	Girls
Pizza	4	3
Burgers	6	6
Fish cakes	2	3
Sausages	7	6
Salad	1	12
Total	20	30

a What percentage of the children surveyed preferred pizza?

_____

`1 mark`

b Which lunch did 10% of the boys prefer? _____

`1 mark`

c Which lunch did 40% of the girls prefer? _____

`1 mark`

d Alex said, 'My survey shows that burgers are just as popular with girls as with boys'. Explain why Alex is wrong.

_____

_____

`1 mark`

e Which lunch is equally popular with boys and girls? _____

`1 mark`

2 A clothes shop is having a sale.
All clothes are reduced by 20%.

a What is the sale price of a jacket normally priced at £60?

_____

`1 mark`

b What is the sale price of a shirt normally priced at £32?

_____

`1 mark`

c On the last day of the sale, the **sale price** is reduced by a further 10%.
Which of the following is the last day price of a pair of boots normally priced at £100? Tick the correct answer.

☐ £80   ☐ £70   ☐ £72   ☐ £90

`1 mark`

3 The table shows the 2005 population of each of the world's continents.

Continent	Population (in millions)
Australasia	33
Africa	841
Asia	3825
Europe	735
North America	492
South America	379
World total	**6305**

a Which continent had about 6% of the world's population in 2005?

_____

1 mark

b In 2005, what percentage of the world's population was living in Africa?

_____

2 marks

4 The pie chart shows how a farmer uses his land.
The angle for fallow land is 45°.

a What percentage of the farm is fallow land?

_____

1 mark

Crops

Cattle

Fallow land

b 330 acres are used for crops. What is the
total acreage of the farm?

_____

2 marks

c Next year the farmer plans to decrease the acreage for cattle
by $33\frac{1}{3}$ % and increase the amount for crops by $33\frac{1}{3}$ %.
Tick the statement that is true.

☐ The amount of fallow land will stay the same.

☐ The amount of fallow land will increase.

☐ The amount of fallow land will decrease.

☐ You cannot tell how the amount of fallow land will change.

1 mark

levels
5-6

1 a Write the ratio 6 : 9 in its simplest form. _____

1 mark

b Write the ratio 15 : 25 in its simplest form. _____

1 mark

2 The ratio of two packets of cornflakes is 3 : 4. Find the mass of the larger packet.

_____

2 marks

3 Shade the diagram so that the ratio of shaded squares to unshaded squares is 1 : 3

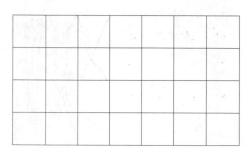

1 mark

4 a Divide £90 in the ratio 1 : 4 _____

2 marks

b Divide 150 kg in the ratio 2 : 3 _____

2 marks

5 A drink is made from cranberry juice and lemonade in the ratio 2 : 7

a How much lemonade is needed if 50 ml of cranberry juice is used?

_____

2 marks

b How much cranberry juice is in 450 ml of the drink?

_____

2 marks

6 The diagram shows a grey rectangle
8 cm by 6 cm with a black square
3 cm by 3 cm drawn inside it.

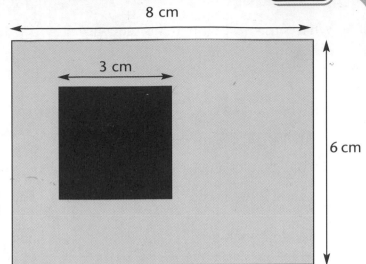

8 cm

3 cm

6 cm

a Calculate the ratio of the perimeter of
the rectangle to the perimeter of the
square. Give your answer in its
simplest form.

_____ **2 marks**

b Calculate the ratio
grey area : black area
Give your answer in its simplest form.

_____ **2 marks**

7 Fatima won £146 on the lottery.

She decided to start two bank accounts for her grandchildren, Nadia, aged 3 years old
and Naseem, aged 5.

She shared the money between the children in the ratio of their ages.

a How much did each child get in the bank? _____ **2 marks**

b The following year she won another £146 and did the same thing with the money.

How much would each child have in the bank in total now?

_____ **2 marks**

8 A fizzy drink is sold in two sizes. The small bottle
costs 35p and the larger bottle costs 60p.

a Write down the ratio of the sizes of the bottles in
its simplest form. _____ **1 mark**

b Write down the ratio of the costs of the bottles in
its simplest form. _____ **1 mark**

c Which size is the best value for money?

Explain your answer. _____ **2 marks**

FRUIT
FIZZ
250 ml

FRUIT
FIZZ
150 ml

1 What is the next term in this sequence: 4, 9, 14, 19, 24, ... ? _____

1 mark

2 What is the term-to-term rule for this sequence?

7, 11, 15, 19, 23, ...

Tick the correct answer.

☐ add 2 each time   ☐ add 3 each time

☐ add 4 each time   ☐ add 5 each time

1 mark

3 The term-to-term rule for a sequence is 'add one more each time'.
Which of the following sequences obey this rule?
Tick the correct answer. (There may be more than one.)

☐ 1, 3, 6, 10, 15, ...

☐ 1, 3, 6, 9, 12, ...

☐ 5, 7, 10, 14, 19, ...

☐ 100, 99, 97, 94, 90, ...

1 mark

4 What is the next number in this sequence: 10, 7, 4, 1, –2, ... ? _____ **1 mark**

5 A sequence has the term-to-term rule 'multiply by 2 and add 1'.
Which of these series of three terms could be in the sequence?
Tick the correct answer. (There may be more than one.)

☐ 1, 3, 5, ...

☐ 2, 5, 11, ...

☐ 10, 21, 63, ...

☐ –3, –5, –9, ...

1 mark

6 The *n*th term of a sequence is 2*n* – 1.

Write down the first three terms of the sequence. _____

2 marks

7 Look at this series of patterns.

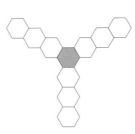
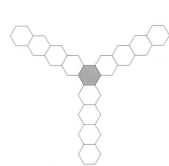

Pattern 1

Pattern 2

Pattern 3

Pattern 4

a How many grey hexagons will there be in Pattern 6?

_____

1 mark

b What is the *n*th term of the sequence for the number of white hexagons?

_____

1 mark

8 Look at this series of patterns.

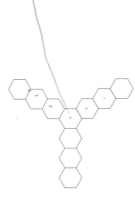
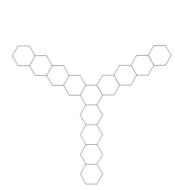

Pattern 1

Pattern 2

Pattern 3

Pattern 4

What is the *n*th term of the number of hexagons in this sequence?

_____

2 marks

9 What is the missing term in this sequence?

3, 4, ... , 12, 19, 28, 39, 52   _____

1 mark

10 What is the *n*th term in this sequence?

8, 12, 16, 20, 24, ...   _____

2 marks

ALGEBRA

Multiples, factors, square numbers and primes

1 What are the first 3 multiples of 7? _____ , _____ , _____

1 mark

2 What is the nth term of the series: 1, 4, 9, 16, 25, ... ? _____

1 mark

3 Which of these statements are true and which are false?
Tick the correct box for each statement.

	True	False
If $x^2 = 64$, then x must equal 8.	☐	☐
All numbers have an even number of factors.	☐	☐
81 is a square number.	☐	☐
1 is a factor of all numbers.	☐	☐
Numbers with only 2 factors are called prime numbers.	☐	☐
All prime numbers are odd.	☐	☐

6 marks

4 Write down the factors of 24. _____

2 marks

5 What is the highest common factor of 24 and 64? _____

1 mark

6 What is the lowest common multiple of 9 and 12? _____

1 mark

7 Which of the following is both a square number and a triangle number?
Tick the correct answer.

☐ 4   ☐ 9   ☐ 25   ☐ 36

1 mark

8 Write down a square number between 101 and 149. _____

9 Here are 10 number cards.

From the cards, write down

a the square numbers _____

b the prime numbers _____

c the factors of 10 _____

10 Circle A contains the first ten multiples of 2.
Circle B contains the first seven multiples of 3.

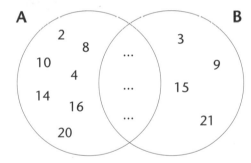

Write down the missing numbers from the overlap.

_____

_____

_____

11 Circle A contains the factors of 20.
Circle B contains the factors of 36.

A

5
10
20
...
...
...
3
12
6
18
9
36

B

Write down the missing numbers from the overlap.

_____

_____

_____

1 Simplify $2a \times 4a$ _____

1 mark

2 Simplify $6a + 7 - 4a + 8$ _____

1 mark

3 If $a = 2$, what is the value of $3a + 7$? _____

1 mark

4 Simplify $2a + 5a - 4a$ _____

1 mark

5 Which of the following are equivalent to the algebraic expression $3n + 4m$?
Tick the correct answer. (There may be more than one.)

☑ $3 + n + 4 + m$ ☐ $6n + 5m - m - 3n$

☐ $12nm$ ☑ $2m + 2m + 2n + n$

1 mark

6 If $a = 3$, $b = 4$ and $c = 5$ which of the following expressions are equal to 27?
Tick the correct answer. (There may be more than one.)

☐ $a(b + c)$ ☐ $a^2 + b^2$

☐ $ab + ac$ ☐ $c^2 + 2$

1 mark

7 Which of the following are equivalent to the algebraic expression $2n$?
Tick the correct answer. (There may be more than one.)

☐ $n \times 2$ ☐ n^2

☐ $\sqrt{4n}$ ☑ $12n \div 6$

1 mark

8 Simplify the following expressions.

a $5a + 6b - 2a - b$ _____

1 mark

b $3a \times 5a$ _____

1 mark

9 Alyssa has a pile of cards.
The total number of cards is $4n + 8$.

4n + 8

a Alyssa puts the cards into 2 piles.
The number of cards in one pile is $3n + 1$.
How many cards are in the other pile?

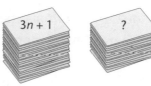

3n + 1   ?

_____

1 mark

b Alyssa puts the cards into 4 equal piles.

?   ?   ?   ?

How many cards are in each pile?

_____

1 mark

c Alyssa counts the cards and finds she has 32 in total.
What is the value of n?

_____

1 mark

10 Look at the rectangle. Write down expressions for the lengths marked **a** and **b**.

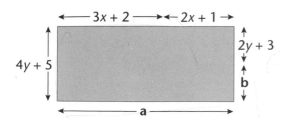

3x + 2   2x + 1
2y + 3
b
4y + 5
a

a = _____

1 mark

b = _____

1 mark

1 The charge for using a gymnasium is

£5 per visit
plus 50p per hour

a How much will it cost to use the gym for 2 hours?

_____

1 mark

b If someone paid £7, how many hours did they use the gym for?

_____

1 mark

2 Which of the following could be a formula that changes 3 into 15. Tick the correct answer. (There may be more than one.)

☐ add 12

☐ multiply by 5

☐ subtract 12

☐ multiply by 6 and subtract 3

1 mark

3 A garden centre uses this formula to work out the cost of a bay tree.

£7 x height of tree in feet plus £10

a How much will a bay tree that is 4 feet high cost?

_____

1 mark

b A bay tree is priced at £27.50. How tall is it?

_____

1 mark

4 The flow diagram shows a formula.

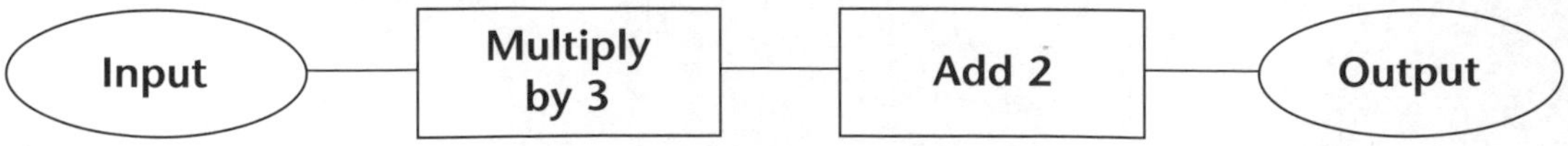

Input — Multiply by 3 — Add 2 — Output

Which of the following pairs of inputs and outputs work for this formula? Tick the correct answer. (There may be more than one.)

☐ input 3, output 15

☐ input 5, output 17

☐ input 1, output 5

☐ input −2, output −8

1 mark

5 Greg is thinking of a number.

I think of a number.
I double it and add 7.
The answer is 12.

What is the number?

_____

6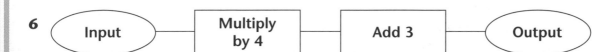

Input — Multiply by 4 — Add 3 — Output

  a What is the output for this flow diagram if the input is 5? _____

  b What is the input for this flow diagram if the output is 5? _____

7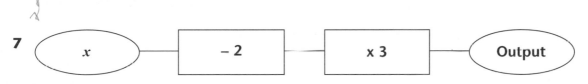

x — − 2 — x 3 — Output

What formula will be the output from this flow diagram?

_____

8 In a sale the prices are reduced by 20%.
This flow diagram shows how to work out the sale price.

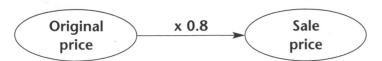

Original price — x 0.8 → Sale price

  a What is the sale price of an item with an original price of £20?

_____

  b What is the original price of an item with a sale price of £32?

_____

1 What are the coordinates of

A (___1___ , ___2___)

B (___3___ , ___−3___)

C (___+4___ , ___−2___)

D (___−3___ , ___4___)

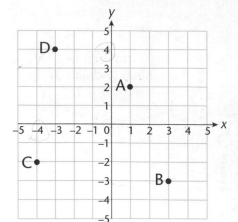

4 marks

2 What relationship do the points
marked on this grid obey?
Tick the correct answer.

$\checkmark$ $y + x = -3$

☐ $y = x - 3$

☐ $y = x - 5$

☐ $x + y = 3$

$(-3, 0)$

$x = -3$
$y = 0$

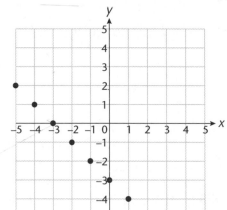

1 mark

3 a What is the midpoint of AB?

_____

b The point C is on the same horizontal
line as A and the same vertical line as B.
What are the coordinates of C?

_____

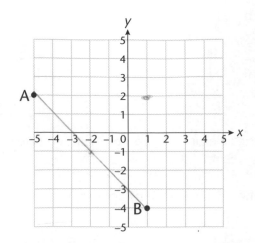

1 mark

1 mark

4 Some points are plotted that obey the relationship $y - x = 5$.

Which of the following coordinates obey the relationship?

Tick the correct answer. (There may be more than one.)

☑ (7, 2)   ☑ (−1, 4)   ☐ (5, 0)   ☑ $(2\frac{1}{2}, 7\frac{1}{2})$

1 mark

5 a A, B and C are three corners of a parallelogram. What are the coordinates of the fourth corner?

_____

1 mark

b X, Y and Z are three corners of a rectangle.

What are the coordinates of the other corner?

_____

1 mark

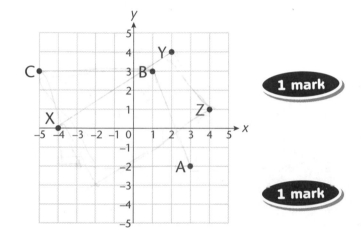

6 Some rectangular tiles are placed on a coordinate grid.

On the first tile, the corner marked with a square has the coordinate (2, 2) and the corner marked with a triangle has the coordinate (0, 1).

a What are the coordinates of the corner with a square on tile 6?

_____

1 mark

b What are the coordinates of the corner with a triangle on tile 7?

_____

1 mark

c What are the coordinates of the corner with a square on tile 20?

_____

1 mark

d What are the coordinates of the corner with a triangle on tile 21?

_____

1 mark

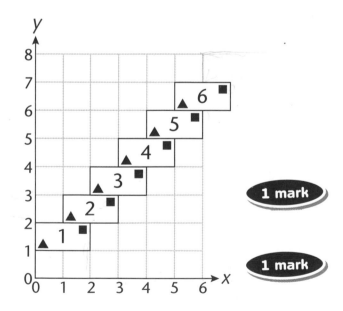

1 What are the equations of the graphs **a, b, c, d**?

a _____

b _____

c _____

d _____

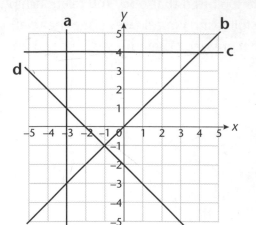

4 marks

2 A is the point (2, 5). B is the point (–3, 5).

Which of the following is the graph of the straight line through A and B?

☐ $y = 2x + 1$ ☐ $y = x + 3$ ☐ $y = 5$ ☐ $y = x + 8$

1 mark

3 The equation of a line is $y + x = 8$.

Which of the following points could lie on the line?

Tick the correct answer. (There could be more than one.)

☐ (–2, –6) ☐ (0, 8) ☐ (–2, 10) ☑ (10, –2)

1 mark

4 At what point do the lines $y = 3$ and $x = 2$ intersect? _____

1 mark

5 Which of these lines passes through the point (–3, 5)?

Tick the correct answer. (There could be more than one.)

☐ $x + y = 8$ ☐ $y = 5$

☐ $x + y = 2$ ☐ $x = –3$

1 mark

6 What are the equations of the graphs **a, b, c, d**?

a _____

b _____

c _____

d _____

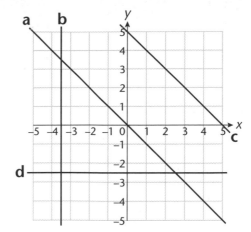

4 marks

7 A, B and C are three corners of a triangle.

  a What is the equation of the line

    i AB _____

    ii BC _____

    iii AC _____

  b What is the area of the triangle ABC?

    _____

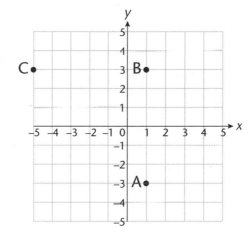

4 marks

8 Draw the following lines on the grid.

  a $y = 1$

  b $x = 2$

  c $x + y = 5$

  d What is the area of the triangle formed by the three lines?

    _____

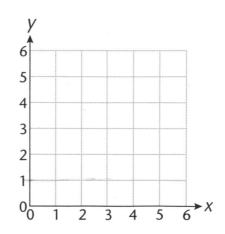

4 marks

1 The equations of four graphs are

$y = 2x + 1$ $y = 2x - 3$ $y = 3x - 2$ $y = 4x + 1$

   a Which two graphs are parallel?

   _____

1 mark

   b Which two lines pass through the same point on the y-axis?

   _____

1 mark

2 Match the lines on the graph with the equations.

   $y = x + 3$ matches line _____

   $y = 3x - 1$ matches line _____

   $x + y = -1$ matches line _____

   $y = -1$ matches line _____

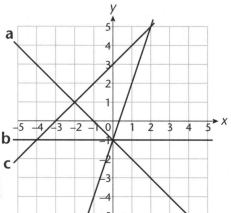

4 marks

3 What is the equation of the line shown?

_____

1 mark

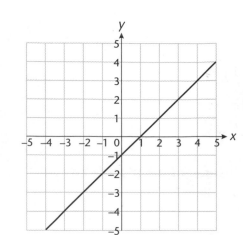

4 A is the point (2, 5). B is the point (−3, −5).

Which of the following is the graph of the straight line through A and B?

Tick the correct answer.

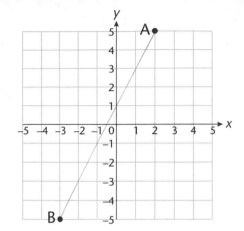

☐ $y = 2x − 1$

☐ $y = x + 3$

☐ $y = 2x + 1$

☐ $y = x − 2$

1 mark

5 The equation of a line is $y = 3x − 1$.

Which of the following points could lie on the line?

Tick the correct answer. (There could be more than one.)

☐ (2, 7)　　☐ (3, 8)　　☐ (−2, −7)　　☐ (−3, 10)

1 mark

6 The solid line on the graph is $y = 2x + 5$.

What is the equation of the line parallel to this line that passes through (0, −2)?

_____

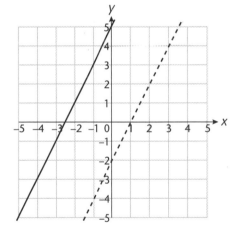

2 marks

7 On the grid, draw the graphs of

a $y = 3x + 1$

b $y = 2x − 3$

c $y = \frac{x}{2} + 3$

d $y = x − 4$

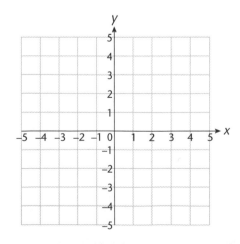

4 marks

1 What is the value of $2n^2$ when $n = 10$? _____

1 mark

2 What is the value of $(2n)^2$ when $n = 10$? _____

1 mark

3 Put brackets in the correct place to make the following calculation true.

$6 - 2 \times 8 \div 4 - 2 = 16$

1 mark

4 Which of the following gives an answer of 20?
Tick the correct answer. (There may be more than one.)

☐ $2 + 8 \times 2$ ☐ $(2 + 3)^2 - 5$

☐ $(5 - 3) \times (3 + 7)$ ☐ $4^2 \times (5 - 1)$

1 mark

5 Work out $6 - (2 \times (8 \div 4) - 2)$ _____

1 mark

6 Work out $5 \times (24 \div 2^2)$ _____

1 mark

7 Work out $72 - 5 \times 6^2 \div 3$ _____

1 mark

8 Work out $(4^2 \div 2) + 3 \times 4$ _____

1 mark

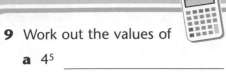

9 Work out the values of

  a 4^5 _____

1 mark

  b 5^4 _____

1 mark

10 Which is greater 2^5 or 5^2? _____

1 mark

11 **a** Work out

    i $10^2 - 8^2$ _____

1 mark

    ii $(10 + 8)(10 - 8)$ _____

1 mark

  b Work out the following.

    i $20^2 - 17^2$ _____

1 mark

    ii $(20 + 17)(20 - 17)$ _____

1 mark

  c Write down the answer to $90^2 - 10^2$.

  _____

1 mark

12 **a** Work out

    i $(4 + 2)(4 + 2)$ _____

1 mark

    ii $4^2 + 2 \times 2 \times 4 + 2^2$ _____

1 mark

  b Work out

    i $(7 - 3)(7 - 3)$ _____

1 mark

    ii $7^2 - 2 \times 7 \times 3 + 3^2$ _____

1 mark

  c Write down the answer to $8^2 + 2 \times 2 \times 8 + 2^2$

  _____

1 mark

1 I think of a number and add three to it. I divide the result by 5 and I get an answer of 6.
What number did I think of?

_____   1 mark

2 Solve the equation $2x - 7 = 20$ _____   1 mark

3 Solve these equations.

a $\dfrac{x - 2}{3} = 7$ _____   1 mark

b $\dfrac{x}{3} - 2 = 7$ _____   1 mark

4 Solve these equations.

a $3x - 8 = 7$ _____   1 mark

b $\dfrac{x + 3}{8} = 3$ _____   1 mark

5 Solve these equations.

a $\dfrac{x + 3}{5} = 6$ _____   1 mark

b $\dfrac{x}{5} + 3 = 6$ _____   1 mark

c $x + \dfrac{3}{5} = 6$ _____   1 mark

d $5x - 3 = 6$ _____   1 mark

6 Solve these equations.

a $\dfrac{x}{6} = \dfrac{7}{4}$

_____ **1 mark**

b $\dfrac{x}{4} = \dfrac{9}{2}$

_____ **1 mark**

c $\dfrac{5}{x} = \dfrac{2}{7}$

_____ **1 mark**

d $\dfrac{9}{2} = \dfrac{15}{x}$

_____ **1 mark**

7 Solve these equations.

a $\dfrac{x}{6} = \dfrac{7}{3}$

_____ **1 mark**

b $\dfrac{x+3}{4} = \dfrac{1}{2}$

_____ **1 mark**

8 Complete the following statements to solve

$$\dfrac{2x-5}{2} = \dfrac{x-4}{4}$$

$(2x - 5) \times 4 = (x - 4) \times$ _____

$8x - 20 =$ _____

$8x -$ _____ $= -8 +$ _____

$6x = 12$

$6x \div 6 = 12 \div$ _____

$x =$ _____

2 marks

9 Complete the following statements to solve

$$\dfrac{4}{x+1} = \dfrac{6}{2x-1}$$

$4 \times (2x - 1) = 6 \times ($ _____ $)$

$8x - 4 =$ _____

$8x -$ _____ $= 6 +$ _____

$2x =$ _____

$x =$ _____

2 marks

ALGEBRA Equations 2

1 Solve the equation $2(x - 7) = 20$

_____ **1 mark**

2 Solve these equations.

   a $3(x + 8) = 21$

_____ **1 mark**

   b $3(x - 8) = 21$

_____ **1 mark**

3 Solve these equations.

   a $4(x - 1) = 6$

_____ **1 mark**

   b $4(x + 3) = 12$

_____ **1 mark**

4 Solve the equation $x - 7 = 2x + 3$

_____ **1 mark**

5 Solve the equation $5x - 8 = 10 + 2x$

_____ **1 mark**

6 Solve these equations.

   a $2x + 5 = x - 1$

_____ **1 mark**

   b $5x - 2 = 2x - 5$

_____ **1 mark**

   c $2(x + 1) = 5x - 1$

_____ **1 mark**

   d $4x + 7 = 6x + 4$

_____ **1 mark**

7 Solve these equations.

a $\dfrac{x+2}{5} = 6 + x$

b $\dfrac{x}{5} + 5 = 3 + x$

c $x + \dfrac{3}{5} = 6 - x$

d $5x - 3 = 6 + x$

8 The following diagram shows a rectangle.

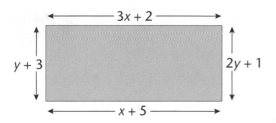

a Find the value of x.

b Find the value of y.

9 The diagrams show some bricks. The bricks on the bottom row add up to the value or expression in the top row.

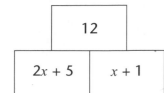

a Find the value of x.

b Find the value of y.

Trial and improvement

1 What is the value of 4^3? _____ ✓

1 mark

2 Estimate the value of 3.1^3. _____ ✗

1 mark

3 Estimate the value of $2.7^3 + 3 \times 2.7$. _____ ✗

1 mark

4 What is the value of $2^3 + 3 \times 2$? _____

1 mark

5 What is the value of $3.2^3 - 2 \times 3.2$? _____ ✓

1 mark

6 A rectangle has sides of x cm and $x + 3$ cm. It has an area of 40 cm².

Which of the following must be true?

Tick the correct answer. (There may be more than one.)

a ☐ $x(x + 3) = 40$ **b** ☐ The sides are 2 cm and 20 cm ✓

c ☐ The sides are 5 cm and 8 cm   **d** ☐ The perimeter is 26 cm

1 mark

7 Complete the table to find a solution to the equation $x^3 = 100$
Give your answer to 1 decimal place.

x	x^3	Comment
4	64	Too low
5	125	Too high

$x =$ _____

3

3 marks

8 Complete the table to find a solution to the equation $x^3 + 3x = 20$
Give your answer to 1 decimal place.

x	$x^3 + 3x$	Comment
2	14	Too low

$x =$ _____

1

3 marks

9 A rectangle has sides of x cm and $x + 2$ cm. It has an area of 16.64 cm².

a Explain why $x^2 + 2x = 16.64$

_____

1

1 mark

b Complete the table to find the value of x.

x	$x^2 + 2x$	Comment
2	8	Too low

$x =$ _____

2 marks

Scales

1 Read the values from the following scales.

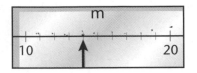

a _____

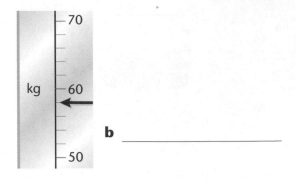

b _____

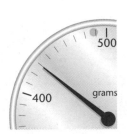

c _____

d _____

e _____

f _____

6 marks

2 A melon is weighed.

A melon and a mango are weighed.

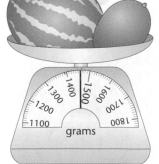

a How much does the melon weigh?
Give your answer in kilograms. _____

1 mark

b How much does the mango weigh?
Give your answer in grams. _____

1 mark

3 How long is there between the time shown on clock A and the time shown on clock B?

_____

Clock A   Clock B

4 The timetable shows bus times from Barnsley to Millhouse.

Barnsley	Kingstone	Dodworth	Silkstone	Oxspring	Millhouse
10:35	10:42	11:03	11:21	11:40	12:00
11:20	11:27	11:48	12:06	12:25	12:45
12:42	12:49	13:10	13:28	13:47	14:07

a What time does the 10:35 arrive in Oxspring? _____

1 mark

b How long does the 10:35 take to get from Barnsley to Millhouse? _____

1 mark

c Jack arrives at Barnsley bus station at 11 o'clock.

i How long does he have to wait for a bus to Silkstone?

_____

1 mark

ii How long does the bus take to get to Silkstone?

_____

1 mark

5 On a visit to his doctor, Mr Sutcliffe has his height measured.

How tall is Mr Sutcliffe? Give your answer in metres.

_____

1 mark

SHAPE, SPACE AND MEASURES

Metric units

this whole topic tu

1 The table shows how much a carrier charges to deliver parcels.

Weight up to	Cost
2 kg	£5.00
5 kg	£8.00
10 kg	£10.00
20 kg	£15.00

Imogen has three packages to be delivered.
The packages weigh 1.5 kg, 4 kg and 8 kg.

a How much do the three packages weigh altogether?

_____ kg

1 mark

b How much will it cost to deliver all three packages?

£ _____

1 mark

c If Imogen puts all three packages together as a single package, how much cheaper will it be to deliver this single package than three separate packages?

£ _____

1 mark

2 A small cola glass holds 125 ml. How many glasses can be filled from a 75 cl bottle of cola?

_____ glasses

1 mark

3 Complete the following metric relationships.

Mass	Volume	Length
$3\frac{1}{4}$ kg = _____ g	650 cl = _____ litres	425 mm = _____ cm

3 marks

4 When Zoe was born she weighed 3 kg 750 grams.
In her first month she put on 450 grams in weight.
How much did she weigh after one month?
Answer in kilograms and grams.

_____ kg _____ g

1 mark

5 Large jars of pickled fruit weigh 650 grams.
They are sold in trays of 12 jars.
How much does a tray of 12 jars weigh?
Give your answer in kilograms.

_____ kg

6 A 1p coin weighs 3.5 grams.
Mohammed has saved a bag of pennies.
The bag weighs 1.4 kilograms.
How much are the pennies in the bag worth?

£ _____

7 Mr Wilson weighs 96 kg.
After dieting he loses $3\frac{1}{4}$ kilograms.
How much does he weigh now?

_____ kg

8 Two bottles together have a total volume
of $2\frac{1}{2}$ litres.
The larger bottle is four times the volume
of the smaller bottle.
What is the volume of the smaller bottle?
State the units of your answer.

_____

SHAPE, SPACE AND MEASURES
Imperial units

1 How many inches are there in one foot? _____

1 mark

2 How many pints are there in one gallon? _____

1 mark

3 There are 16 ounces in one pound.
How many ounces are there in 4 pounds? _____

1 mark

4 1 yard is 3 feet. How many feet are there in 22 yards?

_____

1 mark

5 A crate holds 24 pints of milk.
How many gallons of milk are in the crate? _____

1 mark

6 Approximately how many centimetres are there in one inch?

_____

1 mark

7 Approximately how many litres are there in a gallon?

_____

1 mark

8 Marc buys a 4 kg bag of potatoes for his grandmother and he needs to tell her the approximate weight in pounds.

What is a good approximation for the number of pounds in 4 kg?

_____

1 mark

9 Abigail travels in her car from York to Middlesbrough which is a distance of 50 miles.

She has to convert this distance into kilometres.

What should her answer be?

_____

1 mark

10 Put these weights in order, with the smallest first.

10 oz   600 g   1 kg $\frac{1}{2}$ lb

_____

1 mark

11 A 1p coin weighs 3.5 grams.

Approximately how many pounds does £10 in pennies weigh?

_____

2 marks

12 Mr Stone is 6 feet tall.

Approximately how tall is he in metres and centimetres?

_____

1 mark

13 Two bottles are shown.

Which bottle contains the most?

JUICE
2 litres

ADE 3 pints

_____

1 mark

SHAPE, SPACE AND MEASURES
Measuring angles and bearings

1 How many degrees are there in a complete turn?

_____

1 mark

2 How many degrees are there in a right angle?

_____

1 mark

3 What type of angles are shown below?

a

b

a _____

1 mark

b _____

1 mark

4 Estimate the size of the angles in question 3.

a _____ °

1 mark

b _____ °

1 mark

5 Measure the following angles.

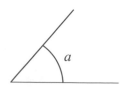 _a_

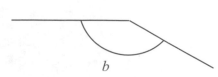 _b_

a _____ °

1 mark

b _____ °

1 mark

6 Draw angles of   **a** 75° **b** 160°

a

b

2 marks

7 Measure **a** the actual distance **b** the bearing of *A, B* and *C* from *O* in the diagram below.

C.

N

Scale 1 cm: 2 km

• *A*

O

B •

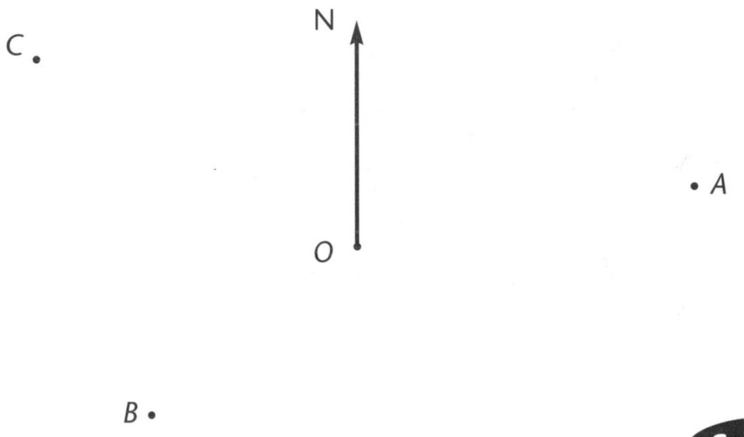

6 marks

8 From the point *O* draw the following points.

N

a   *A* which is 5 cm on a bearing of 065° from *O*

b   *B* which is 4 cm on a bearing of 155° from *O*

c   *C* which is 6 cm on a bearing of 265° from *O*

O

6 marks

Angle facts

1 What is the size of angle *a* in the diagram?

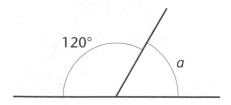

_____ °

1 mark

2 What is the size of angle *b* in the diagram?

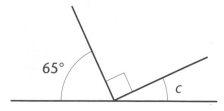

_____ °

1 mark

3 What is the size of angle *c* in the diagram?

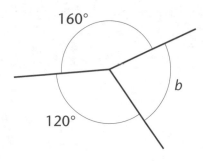

_____ °

1 mark

4 What is the size of angle *d* in the diagram?

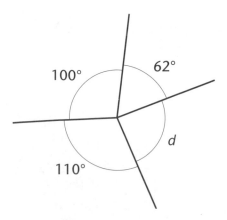

_____ °

1 mark

5 Calculate the size of angle *e* in the triangle below.

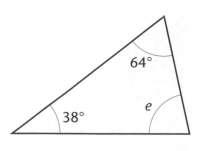

_____ °

1 mark

6 *ABC* is a right-angled triangle. Calculate the value of angle *f*.

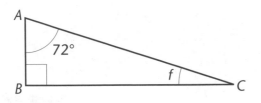

_____°

1 mark

7 *PQR* is an isosceles triangle. Calculate the value of angle *g*.

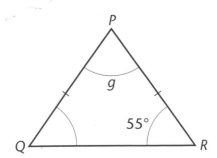

_____°

1 mark

8 Calculate the size of angle *x*.

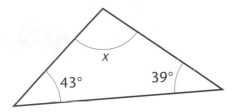

_____°

1 mark

9 Calculate the size of angle *y*.

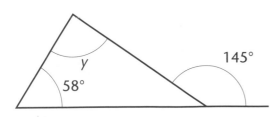

_____°

1 mark

10 Calculate the size of angle *z*.

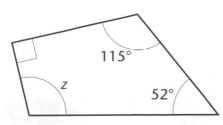

_____°

1 mark

SHAPE, SPACE AND MEASURES

Angles in parallel lines and polygons

1 Write down the values of angles *a*, *b* and *c*.

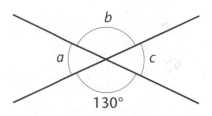

130°

a = _____ *b* = _____ *c* = _____

3 marks

2 Write down the value of angle *d*. Give a reason for your answer.

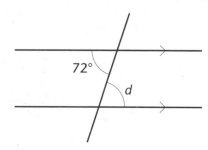

72°

d

d = _____ because _____

2 marks

3 Write down the value of angle *e*. Give a reason for your answer.

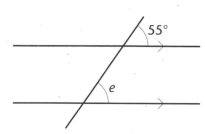

55°

e

e = _____ because _____

2 marks

4 Write down the value of angle *f*. Give a reason for your answer.

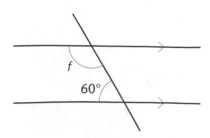

f

60°

f = _____ because _____

2 marks

5 Write down the value of angles *g* and *h*. Give reasons for your answers.

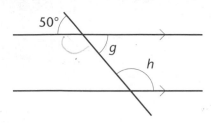

g = _____ because _____

h = _____ because _____

2 marks

6 What is the sum of the interior angles of a pentagon? _____ °

1 mark

7 Which of the following statements is true for a regular hexagon?
Tick the correct answer. (There may be more than one.)

☐ Each interior angle is 60°   ☐ Each interior angle is 120°

☐ Each exterior angle is 60°   ☐ Each exterior angle is 120°

1 mark

8 *ABCDE* is a regular pentagon.
Work out the value of angles *x*, *y* and *z*.

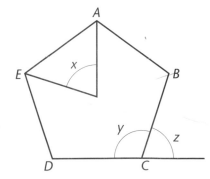

x = _____ y = _____

z = _____

3 marks

9 The diagram shows four regular octagons, A, B, C and D.

Explain why shape S is a square.

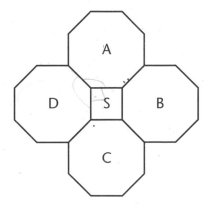

_____

_____

_____

2 marks

SHAPE, SPACE AND MEASURES

Symmetry

1 How many lines of symmetry does a rectangle have? _____

2 What is the order of rotational symmetry for a square? _____

3 How many lines of symmetry does an isosceles triangle have?

_____

4 What is the order of rotational symmetry for a kite? _____

5 Which of the following statements is true for a parallelogram?
Tick the correct statement. (There may be more than one.)

☐ It has no lines of symmetry.

☐ It has rotational symmetry of order 1.

☐ It has 1 line of symmetry.

☐ It has rotational symmetry of order 2.

6 a On the star below, draw on all the lines of symmetry.

b What is the order of rotational symmetry of the star?
Mark the centre of rotation on the diagram.

7 For each of these capital letters, write down **i** the number of lines of symmetry and **ii** the order of rotational symmetry.

a H **i** lines _____ **ii** order _____

b N **i** lines _____ **ii** order _____

c S **i** lines _____ **ii** order _____

d Y **i** lines _____ **ii** order _____

4 marks

8 Shade one more square on the diagram so that it has two lines of symmetry and rotational symmetry of order 2.

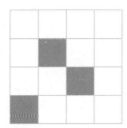

1 mark

9 Look at this series of stars. For each one, write down
  i the number of lines of symmetry
  ii the order of rotational symmetry

a 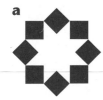 **b** **c**  **d**  **e**

i _____ _____ _____ _____ _____

5 marks

ii _____ _____ _____ _____ _____

5 marks

10 Shade five more squares so that the grid has rotational symmetry of order 4.

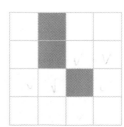

1 mark

SHAPE, SPACE AND MEASURES

Reflections and rotations

1 Reflect the triangle in the mirror line.

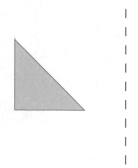

2 Reflect the trapezium in the mirror line.

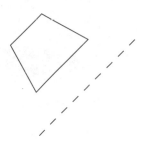

3 Arrow X is rotated clockwise onto arrow Y about the point O.

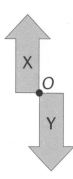

What is the angle of rotation?

_____

4 The rectangle R is rotated anticlockwise onto rectangle S about the point O.

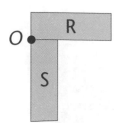

What is the angle of rotation?

_____

5 Shape A is rotated onto each of the shapes B, C and D.
In each case give **i** the angle of rotation
ii the direction of rotation   **iii** the centre of rotation.

B i _____ **ii** _____ **iii** _____

C i _____ **ii** _____ **iii** _____

D i _____ **ii** _____ **iii** _____

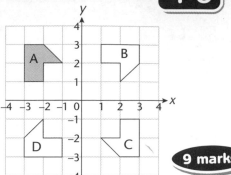

9 marks

6 Shape A is reflected one onto each of the shapes B, C and D.
In each case give the equation of the mirror line.

B _____

C _____

D _____

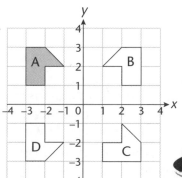

3 marks

7 Triangle *ABC* is reflected in the line $y = x$
onto triangle *A'B'C'*.

a Write down the coordinates of

A (_____ , _____)   A' (_____ , _____)

B (_____ , _____)   B' (_____ , _____)

C (_____ , _____)   C' (_____ , _____)

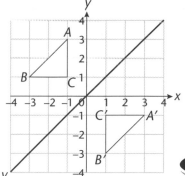

6 marks

b What do you notice about each pair of coordinates
(e.g. *A* and *A'*)?

_____

1 mark

8 Triangles B, C, D and E are all rotations of triangle A.
Match the triangle with the description below.

i Half turn about (3, 5) is triangle _____

ii Quarter turn anticlockwise about (7, 6) is triangle

_____

iii Quarter turn clockwise about (0, 6) is triangle

_____

iv Half turn about (4, 7) is triangle _____

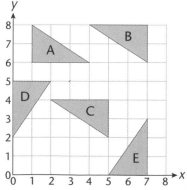

4 marks

SHAPE, SPACE AND MEASURES

Enlargements

1 Shapes A and B are enlargements of the shaded shape.

What is the scale factor of each enlargement?

A _____

B _____

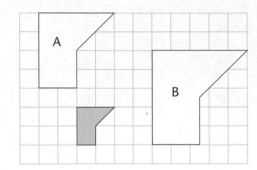

2 marks

2 The white shape is an enlargement of the shaded shape with scale factor 2. One 'ray' joining similar points is shown.

Draw the other rays to find the centre of enlargement.

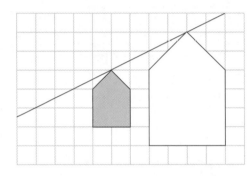

1 mark

3 On the grid, draw an enlargement of the triangle with a scale factor of 2.

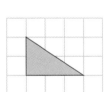
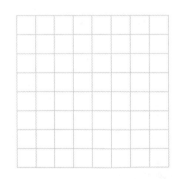

1 mark

4 On the grid, draw an enlargement of the shape with a scale factor of 3.

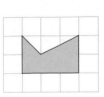
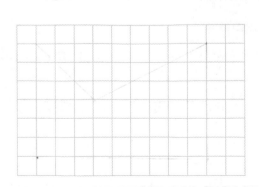

1 mark

5 The triangle *ABC* is enlarged to a triangle *A'B'C'* by a scale factor of 2 about the origin.

Write down the coordinates of the points *A'*, *B'* and *C'*.

A' (_____ , _____)

B' (_____ , _____)

C' (_____ , _____)

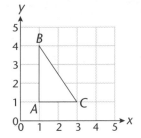

3 marks

6 The triangle *A'B'C'* has been enlarged from a triangle *ABC* by a scale factor of 3 about the origin.

Write down the coordinates of the points *A*, *B* and *C*.

A (_____ , _____)

B (_____ , _____)

C (_____ , _____)

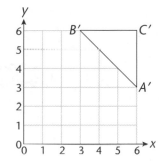

3 marks

7 The shaded triangle has been transformed to triangles A, B and C.

Match the triangle to the transformation described below.

a Enlargement scale factor 2 about (0, 0) is

_____

b Enlargement scale factor 2 about (2, 0) is

_____

c Enlargement scale factor 2 about (4, 2) is

_____

3 marks

SHAPE, SPACE AND MEASURES

3-D shapes

1 Write down the names of these solids.

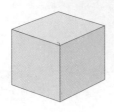 

3 marks

_____   _____   _____

2 How many **a** edges, **b** faces and **c** vertices does a cuboid have?

a _____

b _____

c _____   **3 marks**

3 How many **a** edges, **b** faces and **c** vertices does a square-based pyramid have?

a _____

b _____

c _____   **3 marks**

4 Look at the net.
What is the name of the shape that will be formed by this net?

_____

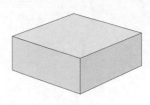

1 mark

5 Which of the following are nets for a cube?

a   **b**   **c**   **d**   _____

1 mark

6 This is the plan and elevation for a solid.
What is the name of this solid?

_____

PLAN   ELEVATION

1 mark

7 For this solid, draw
   a the plan
   b the elevation from X
   c the elevation from Y

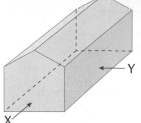

3 marks

8 How many planes of symmetry do the following shapes have?

a 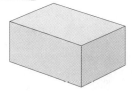   **b**   **c**

3 marks

_____   _____   _____

9 The shape shown is made from six centimetre cubes.
   Draw   **a** the plan
           b the elevation from A

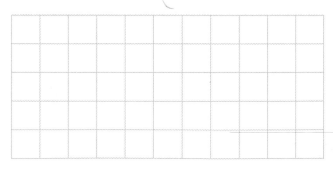
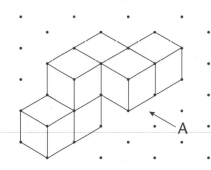

2 marks

10 A shape is made from four centimetre cubes.
    The plan and two side elevations are shown below.

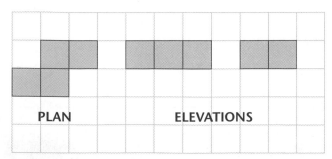

PLAN   ELEVATIONS

Draw an isometric view of the shape.

2 marks

SHAPE, SPACE AND MEASURES
Perimeter and area

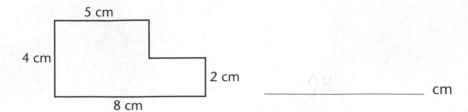

1 What is the perimeter of this shape?

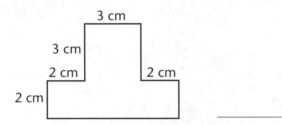

_____ cm

1 mark

2 What is the perimeter of this shape?
Remember to include the units in
your answer.

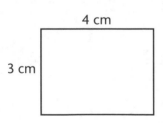

_____

2 marks

3 What is the area of this rectangle?

_____

2 marks

4 What is **a** the perimeter and **b** the area of this right-angled triangle?

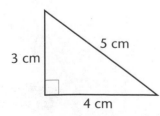

a perimeter _____

b area _____

3 marks

5 Work out **a** the perimeter and **b** the area of this isosceles triangle.
Remember to include the units in your answer.

    a perimeter _____

    b area _____

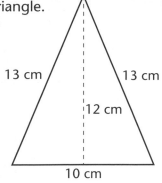

13 cm   13 cm

12 cm

10 cm

3 marks

6 A, B, C and D are triangles drawn on a centimetre grid.
What are the areas of triangles A, B, C and D?

A _____ cm²

B _____ cm²

C _____ cm²

D _____ cm²

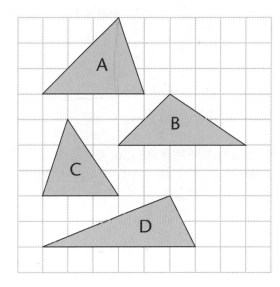

4 marks

7 What is the area of this parallelogram?

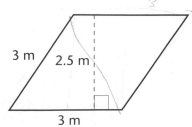

3 m   2.5 m

3 m

_____

2 marks

8 What is the area of this trapezium?

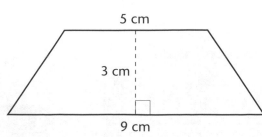

5 cm

3 cm

9 cm

_____

2 marks

Circumference and area of a circle

1 The diameter of a circle is 5 cm.
What is its circumference? Give your answer to 1 decimal place.

_____ cm

1 mark

2 The radius of a circle is 4 m.
What is its circumference? Give your answer to 1 decimal place.

_____ m

1 mark

3 The circumference of a circle is 25 cm.
What is its diameter? Give your answer to the nearest centimetre.

_____ cm

1 mark

4 A tin of beans has a diameter of 7.5 cm.
The label around the tin has an overlap of 1 cm.
What is the length of the label?
Give your answer to 1 decimal place.
Remember to include the units in your answer.

_____

2 marks

5 What is the perimeter of this semicircle?
Give your answer to 1 decimal place.

_____ cm

10 cm

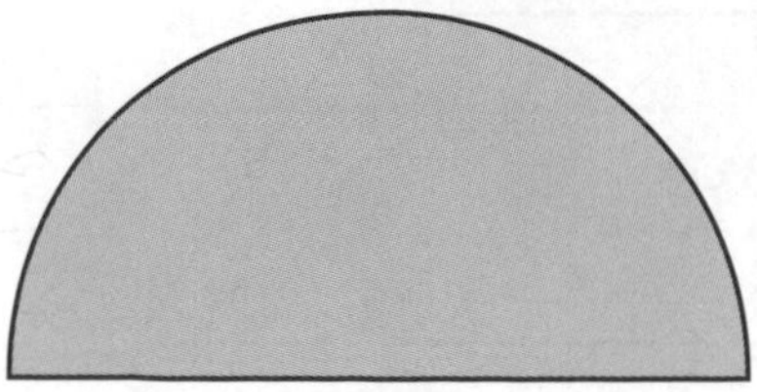

1 mark

6 The radius of a circle is 3 cm.

What is its area? Give your answer to 1 decimal place.

_____ cm²

7 The diameter of a circle is 5 cm.

What is its area?

Remember to include the units in your answer.

_____

8 A circle has a diameter of 18 cm.

What is its area?

Give your answer as a multiple of π.

_____ cm²

9 What is the area of this quadrant?

Give your answer to 1 decimal place.

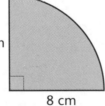

8 cm

8 cm

_____ cm²

10 What is the area of the shaded part of the diagram?

Give your answer to 1 decimal place.

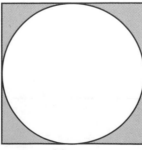

10 cm

10 cm

_____ cm²

SHAPE, SPACE AND MEASURES

Volume

1 What is the volume of this cuboid?

_____ cm³

2 cm

3 cm

8 cm

1 mark

2 **a** What is the volume of this cuboid?

_____ cm³

b What is the surface area?

_____ cm²

5 cm

3 cm

1 cm

1 mark

1 mark

3 A cuboid has a volume of 36 cm³.
Its length is 6 cm and its width is 3 cm.
What is the height of the cuboid?

_____ cm **1 mark**

4 A cuboid has a volume of 200 cm³.
Its length and width are 5 cm.
What is the surface area?
Remember to include the units in your answer.

_____ **2 marks**

5 The volume of a cube is 64 cm³.
What is the length of each edge of the cube?

_____ cm **1 mark**

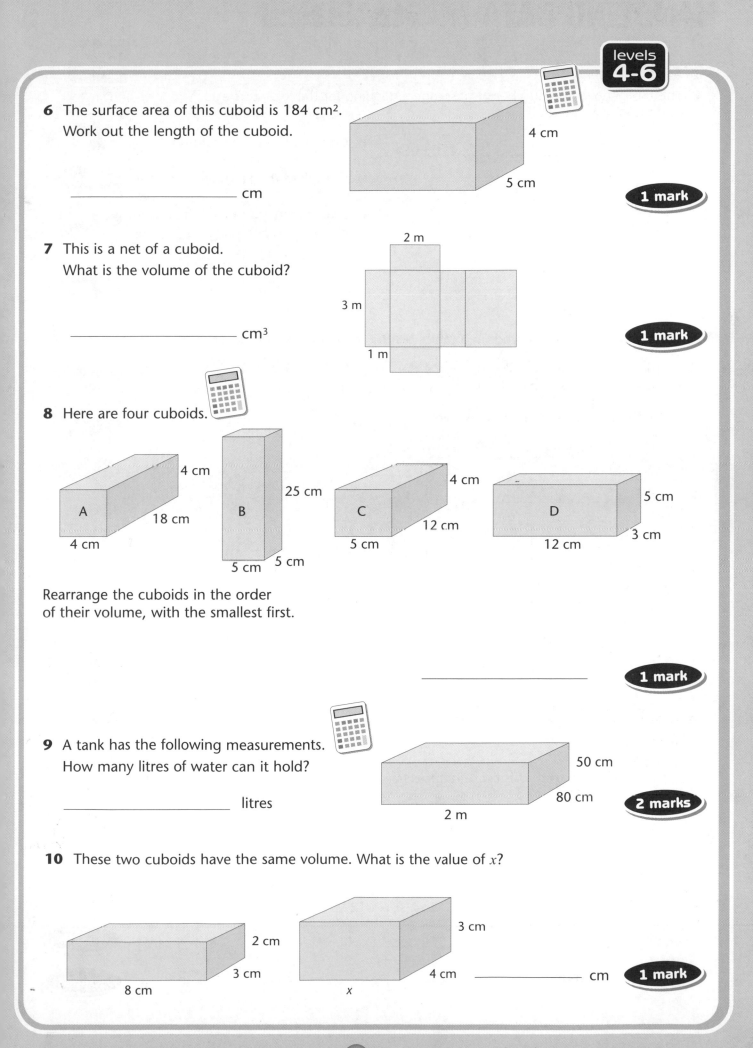

6 The surface area of this cuboid is 184 cm². Work out the length of the cuboid.

4 cm

5 cm

_____ cm

1 mark

7 This is a net of a cuboid. What is the volume of the cuboid?

2 m

3 m

1 m

_____ cm³

1 mark

8 Here are four cuboids.

4 cm

A

18 cm

4 cm

25 cm

B

5 cm   5 cm

4 cm

C

5 cm

12 cm

5 cm

D

5 cm

12 cm

3 cm

Rearrange the cuboids in the order of their volume, with the smallest first.

_____

1 mark

9 A tank has the following measurements. How many litres of water can it hold?

50 cm

80 cm

2 m

_____ litres

2 marks

10 These two cuboids have the same volume. What is the value of *x*?

2 cm

3 cm

8 cm

3 cm

4 cm

x

_____ cm

1 mark

1 The table shows the number of passengers queuing for the local bus each morning for a month.

Passengers	Tally	Frequency
12	||||	4
13	⊬⊬ ||	7
14		8
15		6
16	||	
17	|	

a Complete the Tally column. 1 mark

b Complete the Frequency column. 1 mark

c Explain why you know the month chosen was February.

_____

_____ 1 mark

2 The number of marks scored on a tables test by 30 members of form 9H are:

7 6 5 7 3 5 7 8 9 4 4 10 9 7 5
5 6 10 9 8 7 5 4 7 6 4 8 3 6 7

a Complete the frequency table below. 2 marks

Score	Tally	Frequency
3		
4		
5		
6		
7		
8		
9		
10		

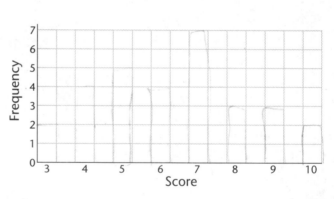

b What was the modal score? _____ 1 mark

c Draw a bar chart to show the data. 1 mark

3 What is the mode from this list of numbers?

2 3 4 3 4 2 5 3 2 4 3 4 5 3

_____ 1 mark

4 The number of marbles in 10 packets is as follows:

11 12 13 11 12 14 17 15 14 12

a What is the range? _____ 1 mark

b What is the mode? _____ 1 mark

5 The ages of a junior hockey team are as follows:

13 14 12 14 12 14 9 13 12 10 12

   a What is the modal age? _____

   b What is the range of the ages? _____

6 This frequency table shows the number of visits to the cinema by 30 students over a one-month period.

No. of visits	Frequency
0	8
1	10
2	6
3	4
4	2
Total	**30**

   a Write down the modal number of visits.

     _____

   b Write down the range of the number of visits.

     _____

7 This bar chart shows the midday temperature in London during one month.

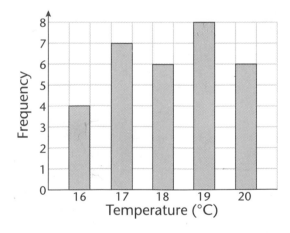

   a For how many days was the temperature recorded? _____

   b What is the modal temperature? _____

   c What is the range of the temperature? _____

   d The month recorded was either July or January.
     Which was it?

     _____

HANDLING DATA

Mode, median and mean

levels
3-6

1 What is the median for this list of numbers?

5   10   8   8   5   4   8   6   7

_____

1 mark

2 What is the mean for this set of numbers?

23   32   42   38   21   26   30   28   _____

1 mark

3 The number of sweets in 10 packets are as follows:

34   35   36   37   38   38   38   39   39   40

Work out **a** the mode, **b** the median and **c** the mean.

a _____

1 mark

b _____

1 mark

c _____

1 mark

4 The ages of a football team are as follows:

23   24   22   24   18   24   19   23   26   20   19

Work out **a** the mode, **b** the median and **c** the mean.

a _____

1 mark

b _____

1 mark

c _____

1 mark

5 This frequency table shows the number of letters in 40 words taken from a passage in a magazine. Work out **a** the mode, **b** the median and **c** the mean.

No. of letters	Frequency
1	4
2	5
3	9
4	7
5	6
6	6
7	3
Total	40

a _____

1 mark

b _____

1 mark

c _____

1 mark

6 This bar chart shows the number of merits in a week for a class of Year 9 students.

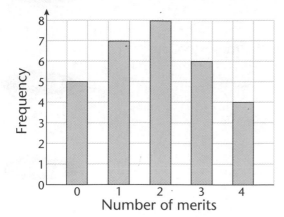

a How many students are in the class?

_____

b What is the modal number of merits?

_____

c What is the total number of merits?

_____

d What is the mean number of merits?

_____

7 This grouped frequency table shows the ages of 50 members of a tennis club.

Which of the following statements could be true and which must be false?

Age	Frequency
21 – 30	15
31 – 40	18
41 – 50	12
51 – 60	4
61 – 70	1
Total	50

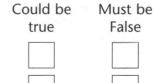

	Could be true	Must be False
a The median age is 45.	☐	☐
b The modal age is 65.	☐	☐
c The modal age is 49.	☐	☐

8 The bar charts show the number of days absent in a week for students in two different classes in Year 10.

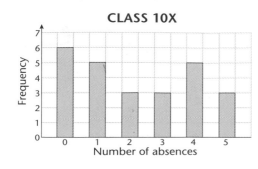

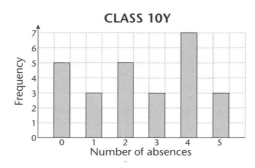

a State the modal number of absences for each class. 10X _____ 10Y _____

b Work out the median number of absences for each class. 10X_____ 10Y _____

c Work out the mean number of absences for each class. 10X _____ 10Y _____

d Which class was worse for absentees? Give a reason for your answer.

_____

HANDLING DATA

Comparing distributions

1 The table shows information about two sets of data.

	Mean	Range
Set A	12	8
Set B	12	3

Which set is the more consistent?

_____

2 Find three numbers with a mode of 6 and a mean of 7. _____

3 Find three numbers with a median of 5, a mean of 6 and a range of 5.

_____

4 Three numbers have a mode of 8 and a range of 6.
Write down two possible sets of data for which this is possible.

_____ and _____

5 The table shows information about how late two buses are over a 20-day period.
The data is in minutes.

	Mean	Median	Mode	Range
Bus A	8	9	3	15
Bus B	8	4	0	10

Which bus is the most reliable?
Give a reason for your answer.

_____

_____

6 The following data shows the weekly wages in a small factory with 8 workers.

£95   £220   £220   £220   £220   £220   £320   £700

Which of the following is true for the data?
Tick the correct answer. (There may be more than one.)

a ☐ The mean is not a good average to use as it is affected by the large value.

b ☐ The mode is a representative average.

c ☐ The range of £605 shows that there are a wide variety of different wages in the factory.

d ☐ The range of £605 shows that the data is inconsistent.

7 The following data shows the weekly wages in a small factory with 8 workers.

£95   £220   £220   £220   £220   £220   £320   £700

Everyone gets a £20 a week pay rise.

Which of the following is true for the new wages?

Tick the correct answer. (There may be on more than one.)

a ☐ The mean will increase by £20.

b ☐ The mode will increase by £20.

c ☐ The median will increase by £20.

d ☐ The range will increase by £20.

1 mark

8 Two girls want to be in the school senior netball team.

The number of goals they scored in their last 10 junior matches was:

Aisha   3   7   2   4   4   1   1   0   2   1

Sarah   3   4   2   3   3   1   2   2   3   2

a Work out the mean number of goals for each girl. _____

2 marks

b Work out the range for each girl. _____

2 marks

c Which girl should be chosen for the senior team and why?

_____

1 mark

9 The data shows the number of tomatoes from 10 plants grown in a greenhouse and 10 plants grown outside.

Greenhouse   5   8   7   12   4   6   9   10   8   4

Outside   5   5   8   9   8   6   6   9   8   6

a Work out the mean number of tomatoes per plant for

i the greenhouse _____

ii outside _____

2 marks

b Work out the range for the number of tomatoes per plant for

i the greenhouse _____

ii outside _____

2 marks

c Which is the better place to grow tomatoes and why?

_____

1 mark

HANDLING DATA — Line graphs

1 The graph shows the trend in the temperature in a garden over a week in May. The readings were taken at midday each day.

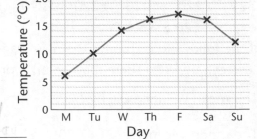

a What was the temperature on Wednesday?

_____ **1 mark**

b The temperature was 16 °C on 2 days.

Which days? _____ and _____ **1 mark**

c On what day was the temperature highest? _____ **1 mark**

d Explain why you cannot tell what the temperature was at midnight on Wednesday. _____ **1 mark**

2 The graph shows the trend in the temperature in a garden over a week. The temperatures were recorded at 12 midday and 12 midnight.

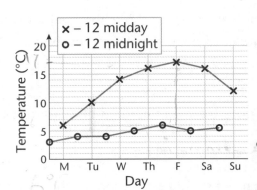

a What was the temperature at midnight and midday on Monday?

midnight _____ midday _____ **1 mark**

b What was the difference in temperatures between midday and midnight on Tuesday? _____ **1 mark**

c Which day had the greatest difference between the temperatures at midday and midnight? _____ **1 mark**

3 The graph shows the miles travelled each month by a lorry driver.

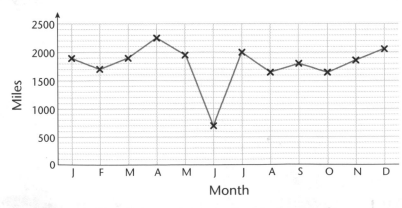

a What was the distance he travelled in January? _____ **1 mark**

b What was the total distance travelled in the first three months of the year?

_____ **1 mark**

c Which month was he most likely to be on holiday? _____ **1 mark**

4 The graph shows the results of an experiment to see if a detergent has any effect on bacteria. Results were recorded every hour from 10 am to 4 pm.

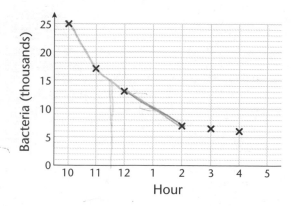

a The scientist was at lunch at 1 pm.

Estimate the number of bacteria at 1 pm.

Give your answer to the nearest 100. _____ 1 000

b When the number of bacteria drop below 5000 the detergent is said to be effective.

The scientist claimed that this graph shows that this detergent is effective.

Is this claim true or false? Give a reason for your answer.

_____ False because the bacteria _____

_____ numbers doln t 5000. _____

c Is it possible to estimate the number of bacteria at 11.30 am?

Give a reason for your answer.

_____

_____

5 The graph shows the depth of water in a drain during a heavy rainstorm.

When the depth gets to 30 cm the area will flood.

John predicts that the area will flood by 2 pm.

Is this claim justified? Explain your answer.

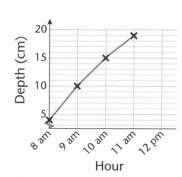

_____

_____

_____

1 This pie chart shows the proportion of boys and girls
in a youth club.

What is the ratio of boys to girls?

_____

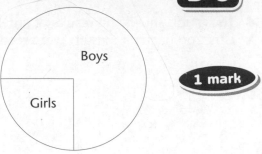

Boys

Girls

1 mark

2 The table shows information on the makes of 36 cars in a car park.

Complete the column for
the angle that each make
would have on a pie chart.

Make	Frequency	Angle
Ford	8	160°
Vauxhall	3	60°
Toyota	7	140°
Total	18	

2 marks

3 The table shows information on colours of cars in a car park.

Colour	Frequency	Angle
Blue	9	162°
White	4	72°
Silver	7	126°
Total	20	

Blue

Silver | White

a Complete the column for the angle that each colour would have on a pie chart. **2 marks**

b Draw a pie chart to show the information. **2 marks**

4 Look at the pie chart which shows the favourite
pets of some students.

Fifty students were surveyed altogether. $\frac{50}{5}$

How many students preferred rabbits?

_____15_____

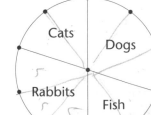

Cats

Dogs

Rabbits

Fish

1 mark

5 Look at the pie chart which shows the favourite
drinks of some people.

48 students chose coffee.

How many students altogether were in the survey?

_____160_____

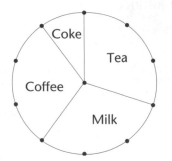

Coke

Tea

Coffee

Milk

1 mark

6 The pie chart shows the results of an election survey.
It is not drawn accurately.
120 people said they would vote Labour.
How many people said they would vote Green?

_____

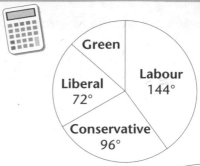

1 mark

7 Which of the following could not be the angles of the sectors in a pie chart?

Tick the correct answer.

a ☐ 90°, 60°, 130°, 80° **b** ☐ 75°, 25°, 200°, 60°

c ☑ 62°, 144°, 96°, 48° **d** ☐ 90°, 90°, 90°, 90°

1 mark

8 Emma did a survey about the month people were born in.
She surveyed 240 people.
Which of the following would be a valid reason why a pie chart is not a good method of representing the data?
Tick the correct answer.

a ☑ There are too many sectors to show a valid comparison.

b ☐ 240 doesn't divide into 360 exactly.

c ☐ People might lie about their birthday.

d ☐ You couldn't fit the labels on the pie chart.

1 mark

9 The table shows information about the nationality of people on a plane.
Draw a pie chart to represent the data.

1 mark

	British	American	French	German
Percentage	45%	25%	20%	10%

10 Draw a pie chart to represent this data.

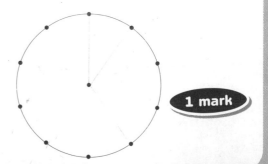

1 mark

Blue	Silver	Black
12	6	2

1 The table shows the heights of some plants in a greenhouse.

Height, h (cm)	Tally	Frequency
$0 < h \leq 10$	⟨⟨⟨⟨ ⟨⟨⟨⟨ ⟨	
$10 < h \leq 20$	⟨⟨⟨⟨ ⟨⟨⟨⟨	
$20 < h \leq 30$	⟨⟨⟨⟨ ⟨	
$30 < h \leq 40$	⟨⟨⟨⟨	

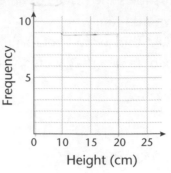

a Complete the Frequency column.   1 mark

b Draw a frequency diagram for the data.   1 mark

2 The frequency diagram shows the marks obtained by a class in a test.

a How many students are in the class?

_____

b How many students got a mark over 50?

_____   1 mark

c If the teacher gave a merit for all students who scored over 85, how many students would get a merit? _____   1 mark

3 This frequency diagram shows the speeds of 100 cars on a motorway. Which of the following statements is true for the data? Tick the correct answer. (There may be more than one.)

a ☐ The average speed is between 50 and 90 mph.

b ☐ The median speed is between 60 and 70 mph.

c ☐ The modal speed is between 60 and 70 mph.

d ☐ The range of the speeds is between 20 and 40 mph.   1 mark

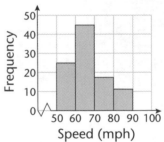

4 The data shows the number of e-mails received over 15 days.

7, 12, 22, 17, 11, 9, 8, 13, 15, 21, 19, 18, 8, 8, 13

Show the data in a stem-and-leaf diagram using the key 1 | 2 represents 12.

1 mark

5 The dual bar chart shows the number of days absences for boys and girls in Years 7 to 11 for one week.

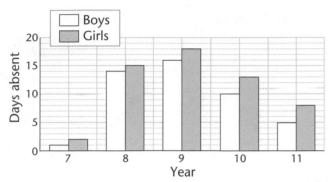

a How many boys in Year 9 were absent? _____

b Which year has the least absence? _____

c How many girls were absent altogether? _____

d How many students were absent altogether? _____

6 The table shows information about lengths of the leaves on a plant.

Length, x (cm)	Frequency
$0 < x \leq 5$	10
$5 < x \leq 10$	17
$10 < x \leq 15$	14
$15 < x \leq 20$	9

Draw a frequency diagram to show this data.

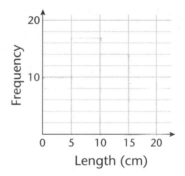

7 The stem-and-leaf diagram shows the ages of 12 members of a chess club.

Key: 1 | 3 represents 13 years.

```
1 | 3   8   9
2 | 0   2   2   2   3   5   8
3 | 1   4
```

a How old is the oldest member? _____

b What is the modal age of the members? _____

c What is the range of the ages of the members? _____

level
6

1 Correlation can be described using the following terms:

S   Strong positive correlation   **W**   Weak positive correlation

N   No correlation

G   Strong negative correlation   **K**   Weak negative correlation

a   Match each diagram with one of the descriptions above.

4 marks

i   **ii**    **iii** 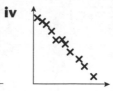   **iv**

b   Match the types of correlation to these comparisons.

   i   The age of a car and its top speed. _____

   ii   The number of men building a wall and the time taken to build it. _____

   iii   The number of ice creams sold and the temperature. _____

   iv   The value of cars and their age. _____

4 marks

2 The scatter graph shows the heights and weights of a breed of horses.

   a   Draw a line of best fit on the data.

1 mark

   b   A horse of the same breed has a weight of 232 kg. Estimate its height.

     _____

1 mark

   c   Another horse has a weight of 200 kg and is 200 cm tall.

     Could this horse be of the same breed?

     Give a reason for your answer.

     _____

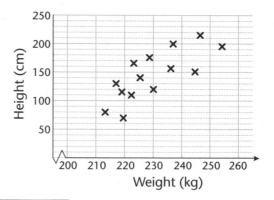

1 mark

3 The graph shows the finishing times of runners in a marathon and the number of miles run per week in training. A line of best fit has been drawn.

  Neil runs 120 miles a week in training.

  What is his likely finishing time?

  _____

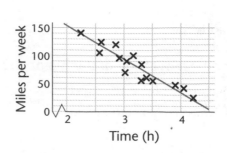

1 mark

4 The scatter graph shows the ages and number of years in the job for the men and women employed in a do-it-yourself store.

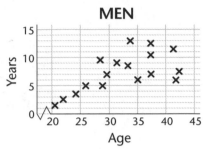

MEN

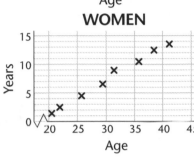

WOMEN

Which of the following statements is true for the data?
Tick the correct answer. (There may be more than one.)

a ☐ The women's scatter graph shows strong positive correlation.

b ☐ The men's scatter graph shows strong positive correlation.

c ☐ There are more men employed than women.

d ☐ For men over 30 there is no correlation between their age and the number of years employed.

1 mark

5 Three different variables are:

A the time it takes to plaster a wall

B the number of men working on a job

C the weekly wage bill

Which of the following will be true?
Tick the correct answer. (There may be more than one.)

a ☐ A and B will show negative correlation.

b ☐ A and C will show no correlation.

c ☐ B and C will show negative correlation.

d ☐ B and C will show positive correlation.

1 mark

6 The scatter graph shows the ages and finishing times in a marathon for 10 members of a running club.

a Describe the correlation.

_____

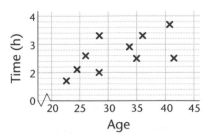

1 mark

b Draw a line of best fit on the data.

1 mark

c Another member of the club is 45 years old. What is his likely finishing time?

_____

1 mark

1 When carrying out a survey, which of the following should you do?
Tick the correct answer. (There may be more than one.)

a ☐ Ask friends, relatives or neighbours.

b ☐ Ask a variety of people.

c ☐ Ask questions that are unbiased.

d ☐ Make sure there is an equal number of boys and girls.

1 mark

2 Jodie does a survey to find out people's views on the following question.
'Should school uniform be worn by all students?'

a Say why each of the following would not be good responses to this question.

i   Yes ☐   No ☐   Criticism _____

1 mark

ii Agree ☐   Don't know ☐   Disagree ☐

Criticism _____

1 mark

iii Ties ☐   Blazers ☐   Shoes ☐   Caps ☐

Criticism _____

1 mark

b Say why this is a good response to the same question.

| Strongly agree ☐ | Agree somewhat ☐ | Neither agree nor disagree ☐ | Disagree somewhat ☐ | Strongly Disagree ☐ |

Reason _____

1 mark

3 Give two reasons why this is not a good survey question.
'People who smoke are not very intelligent. Don't you agree?'

Reason 1 _____

1 mark

Reason 2 _____

1 mark

4 Four students are doing a survey on sport.
Asif decides to ask 30 students in the Badminton club.
Benny decides to ask his Year 9 tutor group.
Colin decides to ask 30 students on the school field at lunchtime.
Derek gets a list of all the students in school and randomly selects 30 names to ask.
Who will get the most reliable results? Give a reason for your answer.

Reason _____

1 mark

5 What is wrong with this question on eye colour?

| What is your eye colour? | **Brown** Yes/No | **Blue** Yes/No |

Reason _____

6 The headmaster gets an alphabetical list of all the students in the school and sends a questionnaire to every tenth name on the list.
Explain why this will give a good sample of the students.

Reason _____

7 In a clothing factory there are 100 women employees and 15 men employees.
The managing director sends a questionnaire to the men and 15 of the women.
Explain why this will not give a representative sample.

Reason _____

8 Jade does a survey to find out people's views on the following question.
'Did you learn anything from the lesson?'

  a Say why each of the following would not be good responses to this question.

  i

  Yes ☐   No ☐   Criticism _____

  _____

  ii

  A bit ☐   Don't know ☐   A lot ☐   Criticism _____

  _____

  iii

  Pythagoras ☐   Trigonometry ☐   Criticism _____

  _____

  b Say why this is a good response to the same question.

  | Mark on a scale from 1 (learnt a lot) to 5 (learnt little) |
  | 1   2   3   4   5 |

  Reason _____

  _____

  _____

9 There are 2000 students in a school.

To find out their views on vegetarianism some students do a survey. Melinda surveys 10 students picked at random from the school roll. Nandi surveys 30 students picked at random from the school roll. Owen surveys 100 students picked at random from the school roll.

Who will get the most reliable results? Give a reason for your answer.

_____

_____

1 What is the probability of throwing a head with a coin? _____

> 1 mark

2 An ordinary six-sided dice is thrown.
What is the probability that it lands on an even number? _____

> 1 mark

3 Here are four events.
  A Throwing a tail with a coin.
  B Snow in June.
  C Walking on Jupiter.
  D High temperatures in Singapore all year round.

Mark each event on the following probability scale.

| Impossible | Very unlikely | Unlikely | Evens | Likely | Very likely | Certain |

0   1

> 2 marks

4 This bag contains 3 white balls and 7 blue balls.
A ball is taken from the bag at random.

  a What is the probability it is blue?

  _____

> 1 mark

  b What is the probability it is white?

  _____

> 1 mark

5 The following cards are placed face down and shuffled.

S T A T I S T I C S

A card is picked at random.

  a What is the probability it is **not** a vowel? _____

> 1 mark

  b What is the probability it is a **T**? _____

> 1 mark

6 In a youth club, the probability that a member picked at random is a girl is $\frac{4}{7}$.
What is the probability that a member picked at random is a boy?

_____

> 1 mark

7 A bag contains 1 blue ball and 4 red balls.

Some blue balls are to be added to the bag to make the chance of picking a blue ball at random $\frac{1}{2}$.

How many blue balls should be added? _____

1 mark

8 A box of toffees contains a mix of nut and plain toffees.

The probability of getting a plain toffee is $\frac{9}{20}$.

What is the probability of getting a nut toffee?

_____

1 mark

9 Here are four events.

A Throwing a three with a dice.

B Picking a vowel at random from the letters

| D | I | S | T | R | I | B | U | T | I | O | N |

C The next person that comes into the room has a birthday in January.

D Throwing a number that is a factor of 24 with an ordinary dice.

Mark each event on the following probability scale.

0                   $\frac{1}{2}$ 1

2 marks

10 This bag contains 4 white balls, 6 black balls and 5 striped balls.

A ball is taken from the bag at random.

a What is the probability it is black? _____

1 mark

b What is the probability it is not striped? _____

1 mark

HANDLING DATA   Probability 2

1 The following cards are placed face down and shuffled.

S T A T I S T I C S

  a A card is picked at random.
  What is the probability it is **not** a letter S or a letter T?

  _____

  1 mark

  b A card is picked at random. It is a vowel. **It is thrown away**.
  Another card is picked at random.
  What is the probability it is a letter **S or T**?

  _____

  1 mark

2 In a church choir, the probability that a member picked at random
is a woman is $\frac{14}{25}$.

What is the probability that a member picked at random is a man?

  _____

  1 mark

3 A box contains 10 coloured balls.

A ball is taken out, its colour noted and then replaced.

This is repeated 1000 times.

The results are Red 822 times, Blue 178 times.

How many red balls and blue balls are in the box?

  Red _____   Blue _____

  2 marks

4 The sample space diagram shows the outcomes
from throwing two coins.

There are four outcomes altogether.

  a What is the probability of throwing two heads
  with two coins?

  _____

  1 mark

  b What is the probability of throwing a head
  and a tail in any order with two coins?

  _____

  1 mark

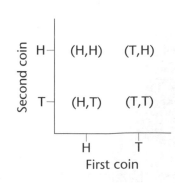

5 Three coins are thrown at once. The outcomes could be, for example, HHH, HHT, HTH.

   a What are all the possible outcomes?

   _____

1 mark

   b What is the probability of three heads?

   _____

1 mark

6 The sample space diagram shows the outcomes for throwing two dice.

   a What is the probability of throwing a 'double', i.e. the same score on each dice?

   _____

   b What is the probability of a score of 4?

   _____

   c What is the probability of a score of 10 or over?

   _____

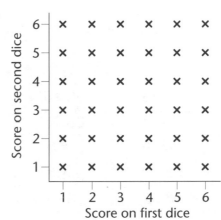

1 mark

1 mark

1 mark

7 This bag contains 4 white balls and 6 black balls.
A ball is taken from the bag at random and then replaced.
Another ball is then taken out.

   a What is the probability both balls were black?

   _____

1 mark

   b What is the probability both balls were the same colour?

   _____

1 mark

8 A four-sided spinner is spun twice.

   a Complete the sample space diagram showing all the possible total scores.

   b What is the probability of getting a score that is

     i even? _____

     ii a square number? _____

     iii a score above 5? _____

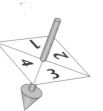

1 mark

1 mark

1 mark

1 mark

		First score			
		1	2	3	4
Second score	1	2			
	2				
	3				
	4				

Practice Paper 1

Time allowed 60 minutes.
You may _not_ use a calculator on this paper.

---

1   The timetable shows the times of the number 32 and 32X bus from Greendale to Oxton.

Stop	32	32X
Greendale	07:55	08:10
Smithies	08:03	08:18
Horton	08:20	↓
Witton	08:32	↓
Oxton	08:52	08:41

a   What time does the 32 bus get to Smithies?

_____

1 mark

b   How long does the 32X take to get from
Greendale to Oxton?

_____

1 mark

c   What do the arrows mean in the column
for the 32X bus?

_____

1 mark

2   Fill in the missing numbers.

a   52 + [_____] = 100

1 mark

b   25 × [_____] = 100

1 mark

c   600 ÷ [_____] = 100

1 mark

d   35 × 2 + [_____] = 100

1 mark

3 Look at the 3-D shapes.

   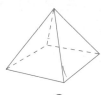   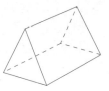

A   B   C   D

a One of the shapes is a triangular prism.
Write the letter of this shape.

_____

1 mark

b How many edges has shape C?

1 mark

c How many vertices does shape A have?

_____

1 mark

4 The diagram shows a rectangle.
Its length is 4.2 cm and its width is 2.5 cm.

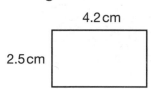

a Two of the rectangles are joined together in different ways to make two new rectangles.

The length of this rectangle is  _____ cm.

1 mark

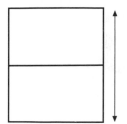

The width of this rectangle is  _____ cm.

1 mark

b How many of the rectangles are needed to make a new rectangle
with a width of 15 cm?

_____

1 mark

5 Reflect each shape in the given mirror line.

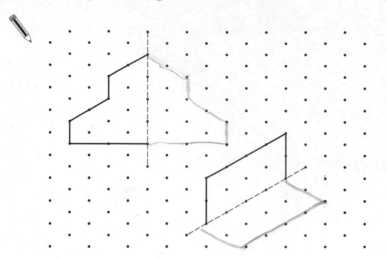

6 Brian buys a computer costing £1040.
He pays a deposit of £200.
He then pays the remainder in six equal instalments.
How much is each instalment?

£ _____

2 marks

7 A litre bottle of lemonade is shared out equally
between five children.
Work out how much each child gets.
Give your answer in centilitres.

_____ cl

1 mark

8 This quadrilateral has one acute angle and three obtuse angles.

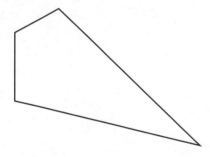

a Now draw a quadrilateral which has two acute angles and two obtuse angles.

1 mark

b Explain why you cannot draw a quadrilateral which has four acute angles.

_____

1 mark

9 a Complete the following sentences.

_____ out of 200 is the same as 40%

1 mark

30 out of 50 is the same as _____ %

1 mark

b Complete the following sentence.

_____ out of _____ is the same as 5%

1 mark

10 Anna buys a box of chocolates that are all the same size and shape. The box contains 12 milk chocolates, 8 plain chocolates and 5 white chocolates. Anna takes a chocolate from the box at random.

a What is the probability that she takes a milk chocolate?

_____

1 mark

b What is the probability that she takes a plain chocolate?

_____

1 mark

c What is the probability that she does not take a white chocolate?

_____

1 mark

11 A single ticket on the metro costs £1.35.
Dave buys a book of 25 single tickets, which costs him £30.
How much does Dave save by buying a book of tickets?

£ _____

2 marks

12 When $a = 6$, $b = 5$ and $c = 2$,

a work out the value of the following:

$a + 2b + c$

_____

1 mark

$3a + b - 2c$

_____

1 mark

b If $a + b + c + d = 20$, work out the value of d.

_____

1 mark

13 Here is a fraction strip.

$\frac{1}{2}$											
$\frac{1}{3}$								
$\frac{1}{4}$					
$\frac{1}{12}$											

Use the fraction strip to help you work out the following:

$\frac{1}{2} + \frac{5}{12} =$ _____

1 mark

$\frac{1}{4} + \frac{1}{3} =$ _____

1 mark

$\frac{3}{4} - \frac{5}{12} =$ _____

1 mark

14 a Complete the table for the mapping $y = x + 5$.

x	2	4	6
y	7		

1 mark

b Complete the table for the mapping $y = 2x - 3$.

x	2	4	6
y	1		

1 mark

c Write down the mapping for this table.

x	2	4	6
y	2	3	4

 $y =$ _____

1 mark

15

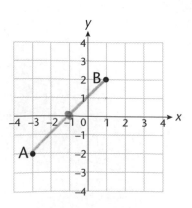

a What are the coordinates of the point A?

(_____ , _____)

1 mark

b What are the coordinates of the mid-point of AB?

(_____ , _____)

1 mark

16 Here are three cuboids.

Cuboid A — 5 cm, 2 cm, 3 cm
Cuboid B — 2 cm, 10 cm, 2 cm
Cuboid C — 2 cm, 7 cm, 3 cm

a Which of the cuboids has the largest surface area?
Tick (✓) the correct box.

Cuboid A ☐   Cuboid B ☐   Cuboid C ☐

2 marks

b Which of the cuboids has the largest volume?
Tick (✓) the correct box.

Cuboid A ☐   Cuboid B ☐   Cuboid C ☐

2 marks

c Cuboid D has the same volume as Cuboid A.
Cuboid D has a length of 10 cm and width of 3 cm.
What is its height?

_____ cm

1 mark

17 Three quadrilaterals are drawn on square grids below.

Quadrilateral A   Quadrilateral B   Quadrilateral C

a Is Quadrilateral A a square? Tick (✓) the correct box.   Yes ☐ No ☐
Explain your answer.

_____

1 mark

b Is Quadrilateral B a kite? Tick (✓) the correct box.   Yes ☐ No ☐
Explain your answer.

_____

1 mark

c Is Quadrilateral C a parallelogram? Tick (✓) the correct box.   Yes ☐ No ☐
Explain your answer.

_____

1 mark

18 Fill in the missing numbers in the boxes.

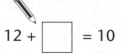

$12 + \boxed{} = 10$

$6 - \boxed{} = 10$

$-2 \times \boxed{} = 10$

19 Work out $\frac{2}{3} \times \frac{3}{8}$

Write your answer as a fraction in its simplest form. _____

2 marks

20 Solve the following equations.

$2x + 3 = 11$ $x =$ _____

1 mark

$3(y - 2) = 9$ $y =$ _____

1 mark

$3z - 4 = z + 2$ $z =$ _____

1 mark

21 15 members of a slimming club record their weights before and after dieting for 3 months. The stem-and-leaf diagrams show the weights before and after the diet.

Before							After						
5							5	4	4	6	9		
6	5	7	9				6	3	5	6	8	4	
7	2	3	6	6	6	9	7	1	2	2	2	9	
8	0	2	4	8			8	3					
9	2	5					9						

Key:

$7 \mid 2$ means 72 kg

Complete the following sentences.

a Before the diet the heaviest person was _____ kg and _____ members of the club were over 70 kg.

1 mark

b After the diet the heaviest person was _____ kg and _____ members of the club were over 70 kg.

1 mark

c Before the diet the modal weight was _____ kg and the range of the weights was _____ kg.

1 mark

22 Rearrange the following equations.

$x + y = 7$ $x =$ _____

1 mark

$3w = z$ $w =$ _____

1 mark

Practice Paper 2

Time allowed 60 minutes.
You may use a calculator on this paper.

1 A clothes shop displays the following items.

£39.99 £85 £34.50 £19.99 £4.49

a Mr Jones buys an overcoat and a shirt.
How much does he pay altogether?

 £ _____

1 mark

b Mrs Smith has £20. She buys two pairs of socks
for her husband. How much change does she get?

£ _____

1 mark

c Frank has £100. Does he have enough money
to buy a jacket, shoes and a shirt?

Yes ☐ No ☐

1 mark

2 This table shows information about pupils in Class 8Q.

Class 8Q	Right handed	Left handed
Boys	8	4
Girls	10	5

a How many pupils in 8Q are left handed? _____

1 mark

b Complete the bar chart to show the number of girls in 8Q.

1 mark

c This is the bar chart for Class 8P. In 8P a quarter of the
boys are left handed and one third of the girls are
left handed.
Fill in the missing numbers in the table below.

Class 8P	Right handed	Left handed
Boys		
Girls		

2 marks

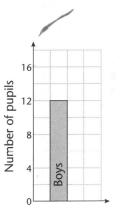

3 Here are some metric units.

kilograms	grams	litres

centimetres	millimetres	centilitres

Fill in the units from the list which best complete each sentence below.

To measure the **width** of a pencil I would use _____

1 mark

To measure the **mass** of a car I would use _____

1 mark

4 Here is a shaded shape on a 1 cm grid.

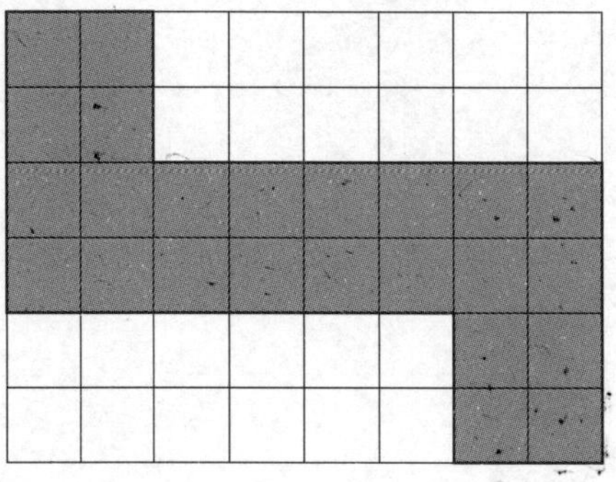

a What is the area of the shape? _____ cm²

1 mark

b The shape is the net of a cube.
What is the volume of the cube? _____

2 marks

c Now draw a rectangle that has the same area as the shaded shape.

1 mark

5 a VAT in Britain is charged at $17\frac{1}{2}$ %.
A camera is priced as £280 excluding VAT.
What is $17\frac{1}{2}$ % of £280? £ _____

2 marks

b In America, sales tax is charged on goods.
A camera costing $120 excluding sales tax had $6.00
sales tax added to the price. What percentage of 120 is 6? _____ %

2 marks

6 Look at these shapes each made from two white cubes and one grey cube.

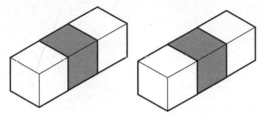

a The two shapes are put together to make a T-shape.
Shade in the faces that are grey.

b The two shapes are put together to make an L-shape.
Draw the L-shape on the grid below.

2 marks

7 The pie chart shows the replies to a survey on holiday destinations.

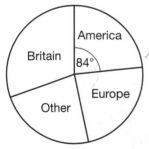

a 7 people answered 'America'.
How many people were in the survey altogether? _____ people

2 marks

b A different survey of 20 people were asked if they preferred staying
in Britain or going abroad for their holidays.
9 people said they preferred to stay in Britain.
On a pie chart, what would the angle be for 'Staying in Britain'?

_____ degrees

2 marks

8 a For each number in the table write a factor of that number that is between 10 and 20.

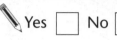

Number	Factor between 10 and 20
48	
150	
51	

3 marks

b Is 150 a multiple of 60? Tick (✓) Yes or No.

Yes ☐ No ☐

Explain how you know.

_____

1 mark

9 The triangle ABC below is drawn accurately.

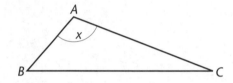

a Measure accurately the angle marked x. _____ degrees

1 mark

b The drawing is a scale drawing of a building plot.
The scale is **1 cm represents 50 metres**.
What is the actual length represented by BC on the diagram?

_____ metres

2 marks

10 Here are eight number cards.

a What is the range of the numbers? _____

1 mark

b What is the sum of the numbers? _____

1 mark

c What is the mode of the numbers? _____

1 mark

d What is the median of the numbers? _____

1 mark

e What is the mean of the numbers? _____

2 marks

11 Here is part of a number grid.

23	24	25	26	27	28
33	34	35	36	37	38
43	44	45	46	47	48

From these numbers, write down one that is:

a a prime number _____

1 mark

b a square number _____

1 mark

c Explain why a square number could never be a prime number.

_____

1 mark

12 a ABC is an isosceles triangle.

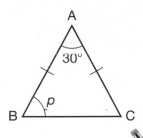

What is angle p? _____ degrees

1 mark

b This diagram is not drawn accurately.
Calculate the size of angle m.
Show your working.

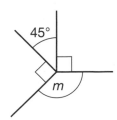

_____ degrees

1 mark

13 A 50p coin has a mass of 8 grams.
How much is one kilogram of 50p coins worth?

£ _____

3 marks

14 The graph shows a straight line.

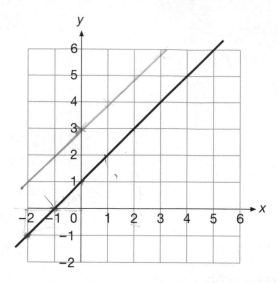

a Fill in the table with some of the points on the line.

(x, y)	(___ , ___)	(___ , ___)	(___ , ___)

2 marks

b Write down the equation of the line. _____

1 mark

c On the graph draw the line $y = x + 3$

1 mark

15 Use your calculator to work out

$(52 + 25) \times (41 - 19) =$ _____

1 mark

$$\frac{52 + 25}{41 - 19} =$$ _____

1 mark

16 A bicycle wheel has a diameter of 70 cm.

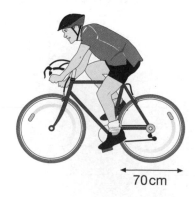

70 cm

a What is the circumference of the wheel?

_____ cm

1 mark

b During a 5 kilometre race, approximately how many times will the wheel turn?

_____ turns

2 marks

17 The standard measure for different paper sizes are
A1, A2, A3 etc. ...
The standard measure for envelopes are C1, C2, C3 etc. ...
All paper and envelope sizes have the width and height
in the same ratio of approximately 1 : 1.4

Ratio of width to
height is 1 : 1.4

a Work out the height of a piece of A4 paper
that is 21 cm wide.

A4 paper has a height of

_____ cm

1 mark

b Work out the width of a C5 envelope that is
229 mm high.
Give your answer to the nearest millimetre.

A C5 envelope has a width of

_____ mm

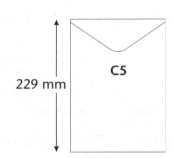

1 mark

c Will an A4 piece of paper, when folded in half, fit inside a C5 envelope?
Explain your answer.

_____

_____

1 mark

18 Some information about the capacity of two football grounds is shown in the table.

	Manchester United	Manchester City
Total capacity	67 500	48 000
Percentage of executive seats	3.4% *2295*	4.9% *852*

Which club has the most executive seats and by how many? _____

2 marks

19 Look at this equation.

$3(2x + 13) = 76 + 4x$

Is $x = 18.5$ a solution of this equation? Tick [✓] Yes or No.

Yes ☐   No ☐

Explain your answer. _____

1 mark

Mental Mathematics Test

Here is an example of a mental mathematics test. Ask someone to read out the questions and write your answers in the book. For the first group of questions you will have 5 seconds to work out each answer and write it down.

Time: 5 seconds

1 Multiply forty-three by ten.

1	

2 How many metres are in 300 centimetres?

2		300 cm

3 What is one-fifth of thirty-five?

3	

4 Subtract four from minus six.

4		−6

5 Look at the equation. When x equals six, what is the value of y?

5		$y = x^2 - 5$

6 What is four point five divided by two?

6		4.5

7 To the nearest ten kilometres the length of a motorway is ninety kilometres.

What is the least value the length of the motorway could be?

7		km

For the next group of questions you will have 10 seconds to work out each answer and write it down.

Time: 10 seconds

8 The chart shows the number of hours of TV watched by a child in a week.

On which day was 3 hours of TV watched?

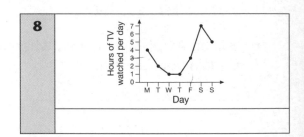

9 A robot moves so that it is always the same distance from a fixed point.

What is the name of the shape of the robot's path?

9	

10 Look at the grid. Write down the coordinates of the point B.

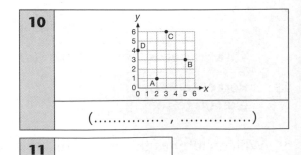

(................ , ...)

11 How many fifths are there in two?

11	

12 Think about the mass two kilograms.

About how many pounds is that?

Circle the best answer on the answer sheet.

12	3 3.5 4 4.5 5

13 Look at the fraction.

Write it in its simplest form.

13		$\dfrac{150}{200}$

14 In a survey one-third of the people asked preferred to go abroad for their holidays.

What percentage is this?

14	

15 What is the area of this rectangle?

<table>
<tr><td>15</td><td></td><td>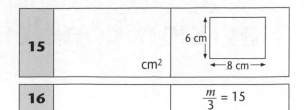</td></tr>
<tr><td></td><td>cm²</td><td></td></tr>
</table>

16 Look at the equation. Solve it to find the value of *m*.

<table>
<tr><td>16</td><td></td><td>$\frac{m}{3} = 15$</td></tr>
</table>

17 The average weight of a male squirrel is 500 grams.

Female squirrels have an average weight that is 5% less than this.

What is the average weight of a female squirrel?

<table>
<tr><td>17</td><td>g</td></tr>
</table>

18 A cardboard box measures half a metre by thirty centimetres by twenty centimetres.

Which of the calculations on the answer sheet will give the volume of the box?

Ring the correct answer.

<table>
<tr><td>18</td><td>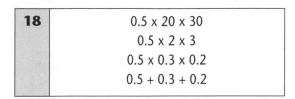0.5 x 20 x 30
0.5 x 2 x 3
0.5 x 0.3 x 0.2
0.5 + 0.3 + 0.2</td></tr>
</table>

19 What is a quarter of two thirds of sixty?

<table>
<tr><td>19</td><td></td></tr>
</table>

20 Look at the inequality.

How many integer solutions are there?

<table>
<tr><td>20</td><td>$3 \le n \le 9$</td></tr>
</table>

For the next group of questions you will have 15 seconds to work out each answer and write it down.

Time: 15 seconds

21 Write down a factor of 48 that is bigger than ten but less than twenty.

<table>
<tr><td>21</td><td></td></tr>
</table>

22 The first odd number is one. What is the hundredth odd number?

<table>
<tr><td>22</td><td></td></tr>
</table>

23 On the grid sketch the line $x + y = 4$.

<table>
<tr><td>23</td><td>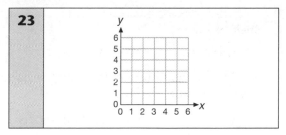</td></tr>
</table>

24 What is the area of a circle with a radius of 3 centimetres?

Give your answer in terms of π.

<table>
<tr><td>24</td><td>cm²</td></tr>
</table>

25 I can make twenty-four different four-digit numbers from the digits one, two, three and four.

How many of these will be odd numbers?

<table>
<tr><td>25</td><td></td></tr>
</table>

26 Look at the calculation.

Write down an approximate answer.

<table>
<tr><td>26</td><td>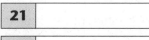$\frac{38.5 \times 51.6}{4.89}$</td></tr>
</table>

27 Complete the factorisation.

<table>
<tr><td>27</td><td>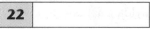$x^2 - 16 = (x + 4)\ (\ ....\ )$</td></tr>
</table>

28 A bag contains only red and blue balls.

There are twice as many blue balls as red balls.

I take a ball at random from the bag.

What is the probability that the ball will be red?

<table>
<tr><td>28</td><td></td></tr>
</table>

29 What 3-D shape has four edges?

<table>
<tr><td>29</td><td></td></tr>
</table>

30 What is the sum of all the integers from 1 to 10?

<table>
<tr><td>30</td><td>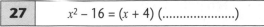1 2 3 4 5
6 7 8 9 10</td></tr>
</table>

Revision checklist

Number

I am able to:

- Recognise the value of a digit in a number ☐
- Apply the four rules to whole numbers and decimals ☐
- Add and subtract negative numbers ☐
- Cancel fractions ☐
- Find equivalent fractions, percentages and decimals ☐
- Find a percentage of a quantity ☐
- Find one quantity as a percentage of another ☐
- Cancel ratios ☐
- Divide a quantity in a given ratio ☐
- Add fractions with different denominators ☐
- Multiply and divide fractions ☐

Algebra

I am able to:

- Give the next number in a number pattern and describe the pattern ☐
- Find multiples and factors of numbers ☐
- Recognise square numbers, triangular numbers and prime numbers ☐
- Simplify algebraic expressions ☐
- Use formulae expressed in words and in symbols ☐
- Find the nth term of a series ☐
- Give the coordinates of a point in any quadrant ☐
- Draw a graph by plotting points ☐
- Recognise graphs of the form $x = a$, $y = b$ and $y = x$ ☐
- Find the relationship between x and y values from the coordinates ☐
- Work out the value of calculations using the rules of BODMAS ☐
- Solve simple equations by rearrangement ☐
- Solve equations where the unknown appears on both sides of the equals sign ☐
- Solve equations using trial and improvement ☐

Shape, Space and Measures

I am able to:

- Convert metric units and imperial units ☐
- Read scales accurately ☐
- Measure angles and bearings ☐
- Calculate angles from known facts ☐
- Recognise line and rotational symmetry ☐
- Recognise the standard triangles, quadrilaterals and other polygons ☐
- Calculate the interior and exterior angles of regular polygons ☐
- Reflect and rotate a shape ☐
- Enlarge a shape ☐
- Recognise the standard 3-D shapes and their nets ☐
- Calculate the perimeter and area of standard shapes ☐
- Calculate the circumference and area of a circle ☐
- Calculate the volume of cuboids ☐

Handling Data

I am able to:

- Collect discrete and continuous data using frequency tables ☐
- Calculate the mean, mode, median and range ☐
- Compare distributions using an average and the range ☐
- Draw and interpret frequency diagrams from discrete and grouped tables ☐
- Draw and interpret line graphs ☐
- Draw and interpret pie charts ☐
- Draw and interpret scatter diagrams and lines of best fit ☐
- Design and criticise questions for surveys ☐
- Understand the likelihood of events ☐
- Mark events on a probability scale ☐
- Calculate the probability of an event ☐
- Calculate the probability of a combined event from a sample space diagram ☐

Workbook answers

Pages 100–101 Place value

1 a Emily
  b 120, 106, 93, 89 *(1 mark for correct numbers in wrong order)*

2 a 299 **b** 2.1

3 a 954, 945, 594 or 549 **b** 165 or 561
  c 514, 516, 546, 564, 594, 596 or 614

4 a Eight thousand and seven **b** 1993

5 a 19 **b** 1.25

6 a 99 **b** 7 (70)

7 6.8, 6.9, 7.0, 7.1 *(1 mark for three correct)*

Pages 102–103 The four rules

1 a 63 **b** 21

2 a 813 **b** 189

3 a 302 *(1 mark for 124)*
  b 195 *(1 mark for 470)*

4 a 163 **b** 297 **c** 740 **d** 111

5

(1 mark if two correct)

6 a £3.15 **b** 24

7 a 18 **b** 19 **c** 34 **d** 555

8 a £9000 **b** £500

9 a 120 **b** 18p

Pages 104–105 Decimals

1 a 1.1 **b** 1.4 **c** 8.17 **d** 19.84

2 a £2.35 **b** 55p

3 a 3.8 or 3.5 **b** 0.3

4 0.1, 1.23, 2.3, 3.21

5 a £3.45 **b** 50p

6 a 40.3 km **b** 5.1 km

7 b < **c** = **d** <

8 b 4.8 **c** 2.7 **d** 0.6

Pages 106–107 Long multiplication and division

Questions worth 2 marks get full marks for a correct answer and 1 mark for correct working with one error. For example, 27 x 32 = 20 x 32 + 7 x 32 = 640 + 214 = 754 would get 1 mark. (The correct answer is 640 + 224 = 764.)

1 a 864 **b** 7812 **c** 34 **d** 71

2 a 816 **b i** 20 **ii** 40

3 a 1196 **b** 19

4 a 360 **b i** 19 **ii** Yes, 19 x 15 – 272 = 13

5 a £2200 **b** £1300 **c** 15

6 19

7 30

Pages 108–109 Rounding and approximation

1 a 370 **b** 400

2 a 4560 **b** 4600 **c** 5000

3 a 5.7 **b** 5.69

4 a 3000 **b** 6 **c** 200 **d** 0.08

5 a About 3 m **b** About 11 m

6 a 50 x 10 = 500 **b** 200 ÷ 40 = 5
                   (1 mark for correct rounding)

7 a $\dfrac{200 + 400}{20 + 10} = \dfrac{600}{30} = 20$
  b $\dfrac{30 \times 60}{20} = 30 \times 3 = 90$
             (1 mark for correct rounding)

8 a 95 **b** 104

9 a Cards are between $7\frac{1}{2}$ and $8\frac{1}{2}$ cm wide.
  b $6\frac{1}{2}$ cm
  c Biggest possible card will fit in smallest possible envelope.

Pages 110–111 Multiplying and dividing decimals

1 a 0 **b** 560

2 a 3400 mm **b** 0.074 m

3 a 0.5 **b** 0.23 **c** 0.006 **d** 100

4 a £68.40 **b** £11.90

5 £37 + £35 + £9 = £81

6 £106.72 *(1 mark for £26.97 or £79.75)*

7 £65

8 a 32.2 **b** 5.9 **c** 41.6 **d** 8.3

9 £42.80

Pages 112–113 Negative numbers

1 a Mars **b** Mercury **c** 710–730 °C

2 a –2 **b** –7 + –6 + –2 = –15
c –7 × 8 = –56

3 a 68 °F **b** –40 °F **c** –20 °C

4 b < **c** = **d** =

5 a –11 **b** 11 **c** –4 **d** 42

6 a Any valid answer, e.g. –3 + –2
b Any valid answer, e.g. –7 – –2

7 a –14 **b** +7 **c** –7, 3

Pages 114–115 Adding and subtracting fractions

1 a £8.25 **b** $\frac{3}{4}$ **c** £8 **d** £32

2 200 125 $\frac{1}{5}$ $\frac{2}{3}$

3 a 1 **b** 21

4 a 17 **b** 10

5 a $\frac{11}{15}$ *(1 mark for $\frac{5}{15}$ or $\frac{6}{15}$)*
b $\frac{7}{20}$ *(1 mark for $\frac{12}{20}$ or $\frac{5}{20}$)*

6 a $5\frac{9}{20}$ *(1 mark for $\frac{9}{4} + \frac{16}{15}$)*
b $1\frac{5}{12}$ *(1 mark for $\frac{11}{4} - \frac{4}{3}$)*

7 a $\frac{5}{12}$ *(1 mark for $\frac{20}{48}$)*
b $\frac{7}{12}$ *(1 mark for $\frac{28}{48}$)*

Pages 116–117 Multiplying and dividing fractions

1 6 **2** $\frac{11}{3}$ **3** $\frac{1}{5}$

4 $\frac{ac}{bd}$

5 $\frac{1}{8}$ **6** $\frac{3}{20}$ **7** 12

8 a 19 kg **b** $\frac{1}{6}$ **c** 19.5 kg **d** 40.5 kg

9 a $\frac{1}{15}$ **b** $1\frac{1}{4}$ **10 a** $2\frac{7}{10}$ **b** $\frac{2}{3}$

Pages 118–119 Equivalent fractions, percentages and decimals

1 b 60%, 0.6 **c** $\frac{3}{4}$, 0.75 **d** $\frac{9}{10}$, 90%

2 a i 6 **ii** 48%
b Any valid answers, e.g. 2 out of 10, 4 out of 20

3 a 20% **b** 40%

4 a $\frac{2}{5}$ **b** 40%

5 a 25% **b** $\frac{3}{8}$ **c** You cannot tell.

Pages 120–121 Percentages

1 a 14% **b** Fish cakes **c** Salad
d 6 out of 20 (30%) is more than 6 out of 30 (20%)
e Fish cakes (10% of each)

2 a £48 **b** £25.60 **c** £72 (10% off £80)

3 a South America **b** 13.3%

4 a 12.5% **b** 880 acres
(1 mark for 330 ÷ 3 = 110)
c Increase. Crops will be 50%, cattle will be $33\frac{2}{3}$ %, so fallow land will be $16\frac{1}{3}$ %.

Pages 122–123 Ratio

1 a 2 : 3 **b** 3 : 5

2 800 g *(1 mark for 200g)*

3 Any seven squares shaded

4 a £18 : £72 *(1 mark for 90 ÷ 5)*
b 60 kg : 90 kg *(1 mark for 150 ÷ 5)*

5 a 175 ml *(1 mark for 25 ml)*
b 100 ml *(1 mark for 50 ml)*

6 a 7 : 3 *(1 mark for 28 : 12)*
b 13 : 3 *(1 mark for 39 : 9)*

7 a Nadia £54.75, Naseem £91.25
b Nadia £113.15, Naseem £178.85

8 a 3 : 5 **b** 7 : 12 **c** Small bottle
(1 mark for 3 ÷ 7 or 5 ÷ 12)

Pages 124–125 Number patterns

1 29 **2** Add 4 each time

3 1, 3, 6, 10, 15, … and 5, 7, 10, 14, 19, …

4 –5 **5** 2, 5, 11, … and –3, –5, –9, …

6 1, 3, 5, … *(1 mark for first 2 correct)*

7 a 1 **b** $3n$ **8** $3n + 1$ *(1 mark for 3n)*

9 7 **10** $4n + 4$ *(1 mark for 4n)*

Pages 126–127 Multiples, factors, square numbers and primes

1 7, 14, 21

2 n^2

3 False, it could equal –8; False, square numbers have an odd number; True; True; True; False, 2 is a prime number.

4 1, 2, 3, 4, 6, 8, 12, 24 *(1 mark for 6 correct)*

5 8 **6** 36 **7** 36 **8** 121 or 144

9 a 1, 4, 9
 b 2, 3, 5, 7 *(1 mark for 2 correct)*
 c 1, 2, 5, 10 *(1 mark for 3 correct)*

10 6, 12, 18 *(1 mark for 2 correct)*

11 1, 2, 4 *(1 mark for 2 correct)*

Pages 128–129 Basic algebra

1 $8a^2$ **2** $2a + 15$ **3** 13 **4** $3a$

5 $6n + 5m - m - 3n$ and $2m + 2m + 2n + n$

6 $a(b + c)$, $ab + ac$ and $c^2 + 2$

7 $n \times 2$ and $12n \div 6$

8 a $3a + 5b$ **b** $15a^2$

9 a $n + 7$ **b** $n + 2$ **c** 6

10 a $= 5x + 3$ **b** $= 2y + 2$

Pages 130–131 Formulae

1 a £6 **b** 4 hours

2 Add 12, Multiply by 5 and Multiply by 6 and subtract 3.

3 a £38 **b** 2.5 feet

4 a Input 5, output 17 and Input 1, output 5

5 2.5

6 a 23 **b** 0.5

7 $3(x - 2)$

8 a £16 **b** £40

Pages 132–133 Coordinates

1 A(1, 2), B(3, –2), C(–4, –2), D(–3, 4)

2 $y + x = -3$

3 a (–2, –1) **b** (1, 2)

4 (–1, 4) and $(2\frac{1}{2}, 7\frac{1}{2})$

5 a (–3, –2) **b** (–2, –3)

6 a (7, 7) **b** (6, 7) **c** (21, 21)
 d (20, 21)

Pages 134–135 Drawing graphs

1 a $x = -3$ **b** $y = x$ **c** $y = 4$ **d** $x + y = -2$

2 $y = 5$

3 (0, 8), (–2, 10) and (10, –2)

4 (2, 3)

5 $y = 5$, $x + y = 2$ and $x = -3$

6 a $y = -x$ **b** $x = -3$ **c** $x + y = 5$
 d $y = -2$

7 a i $x = 1$ **ii** $y = 3$ **iii** $x + y = -2$
 b 18 square units

8 **d** 2 square units

Pages 136–137 Linear graphs

1 a $y = 2x + 1$ and $y = 2x - 3$
 b $y = 2x + 1$ and $y = 4x + 1$

2 c, d, a, b **3** $y = x - 1$

4 $y = 2x + 1$ **5** (3, 8) and (–2, –7)

6 $y = 2x - 2$

7

Pages 138–139 BODMAS and powers

1 200

2 400

3 $(6 - 2) \times 8 \div (4 - 2)$

4 $(2 + 3)^2 - 5$ and $(5 - 3) \times (3 + 7)$

5 4

6 30

7 12

8 20

9 a 1024 **b** 625

10 2^5, as $2^5 = 32$ and $5^2 = 25$

11 a i 36 **ii** 36 **b i** 111 **ii** 111
  c 8000

12 a i 36 **ii** 36 **b i** 16 **ii** 16 **c** 100

Pages 140–141 Equations 1

1 27

2 13.5

3 a 23 **b** 27

4 a 5 **b** 21

5 a 27 **b** 15 **c** 5.4 **d** 1.8

6 a 10.5 **b** 18 **c** 17.5 **d** $3\frac{1}{3}$

7 a 14 **b** −1

8 $(2x - 5) \times 4 = (x - 4) \times 2$

$$8x - 20 = 2x - 8$$
$$8x - 2x = -8 + 20$$
$$6x = 12$$
$$6x \div 6 = 12 \div 6$$
$$x = 2$$

(1 mark for 3 correct lines)

9 $\dfrac{4}{x + 1} = \dfrac{6}{2x + 1}$

$$4 \times (2x - 1) = 6 \times (x + 1)$$
$$8x - 4 = 6x + 6$$
$$8x - 6x = 6 + 4$$
$$2x = 10$$
$$x = 5$$

(1 mark for 3 correct lines)

Pages 142–143 Equations 2

1 17 **2 a** −1 **b** 15

3 a 2.5 **b** 0 **4** −10

5 6 **6 a** −6 **b** −1 **c** 1 **d** 1.5

7 a −7 **b** 2.5 **c** 2.7 **d** 2.25

8 a 1.5 **b** 2 **9 a** 2 **b** −5

Pages 144–145 Trial and improvement

1 64 **2** 30 **3** 30–35

4 14 **5** 26.368

6 $x(x + 3) = 40$, sides are 5 cm and 8 cm and perimeter is 26 cm.

7 4.6 *(1 mark for testing a value between 4 and 5, 1 mark for testing 4.65)*

8 2.3 *(1 mark for testing a value between 2 and 3, 1 mark for testing 2.35)*

9 a Area = $x(x + 2) = x^2 + 2x = 16.64$ **b** 3.2 *(1 mark for testing value above 2)*

Pages 146–147 Scales

1 a 14 m **b** 58 kg **c** 430 grams
  d 5.1 cm **e** 75 mph **f** 64 litres

2 a 1.1 kg **b** 360 g **3** 3 h 55 m

4 a 11:40 **b** 1 h 25 m
  c i 20 m **ii** 46 m

5 1.62 cm

Pages 148–149 Metric units

1 a 13.5 kg **b** £23 **c** £8

2 6

3 a 3250 g **b** 6.5 l **c** 42.5 cm

4 4 kg 200 g

5 7.8 kg *(1 mark for 7800 g)*

6 £4 *(1 mark for 400)*

7 $92\frac{3}{4}$ kg

8 0.5 litres or 50 cl or 500 ml
  (1 mark for value, 1 mark for units)

Pages 150–151 Imperial units

1 12   **2** 8   **3** 64   **4** 66

5 3   **6** 2.5   **7** 4.5

8 8.5 to 9 pounds   **9** 80 km

10 $\frac{1}{2}$ lb, 10 oz, 600 g, 1 kg

11 8 pounds *(1 mark for 3.5 kg)*

12 1 m 80 cm   **13** 2 litres ≈ 3.5 pints

Pages 152–153 Measuring angles and bearings

1 360°

2 90°

3 a Acute   **b** Reflex

4 a 35–45°   **b** 275–285°

5 a 50°   **b** 150°

6 a

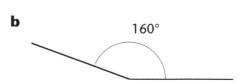

75°

b

160°

7 a *A* is 9 km, *B* is 7 km, *C* is 10 km
b *A* is 080°, *B* is 230°, *C* is 300°

8 *Shown half scale*

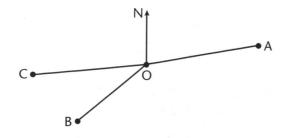

Pages 154–155 Angle facts

1 60°   **2** 80°   **3** 25°   **4** 88°

5 78°   **6** 18°   **7** 70°   **8** 98°

9 87°   **10** 103°

Pages 156–157 Angles in parallel lines and polygons

1 *a* = 50° *b* = 130° *c* = 50°

2 *d* = 72° because alternate angles

3 *e* = 55° because corresponding angles

4 *f* = 120° because allied angles

5 *g* = 50° because (vertically) opposite angles, *h* = 130° because allied angles

6 540°

7 Each interior angle is 120° and Each exterior angle is 60°

8 *x* = 72° *y* = ~~144°~~ 108 *z* = 72°

9 Angles at any corner are 90° = 360° – 135° – 135° and all sides equal

Pages 158–159 Symmetry

1 2   **2** 4

3 1   **4** 1

5 It has no lines of symmetry and It has rotational symmetry of order 2

6 a

b 5

7 a i 2 **ii** 2
  b i 0 **ii** 2
  c i 0 **ii** 2
  d i 1 **ii** 1

8

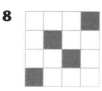

9 i 8, 0, 7, 6, 4 **ii** 8, 6, 7, 6, 4

10

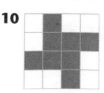

Pages 160–161 Reflections and rotations

1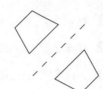

2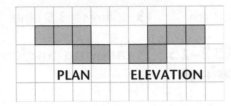

3 180°

4 270°

5 i B 90° **C** 180° **D** 270° (reversed if all anticlockwise) **ii** All clockwise **iii** All origin

6 B y-axis **C** y = x **D** x-axis

7 a A(–1, 3): A'(3, –1) B(–3, 1): B'(1, –3) C(–1, 1): C'(1, –1) **b** x- and y-coordinates have swapped over.

8 i C **ii** E **iii** D **iv** B

Pages 162–163 Enlargements

1 A 2 B 2½

2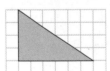

3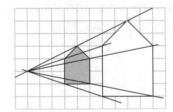

4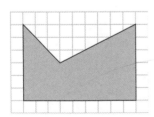

5 A'(2, 2), B'(2, 8), C'(6, 2)

6 A(2, 1), B(1, 2), C(2, 2)

7 a B **b** A **c** C

Pages 164–165 3-D shapes

1 Cube Cylinder Cuboid

2 a 12 **b** 6 **c** 8

3 a 8 **b** 5 **c** 5

4 Triangular prism **5** a, b and c

6 Square-based pyramid

7 a **b** **c**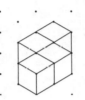

8 a 3 **b** Infinite **c** 7

9

PLAN   ELEVATION

10

(1 mark for any isometric diagram with 4 cubes)

Pages 166–167 Perimeter and area

1 24 cm

2 24 cm *(1 mark for units)*

3 12 cm² *(1 mark for units)*

4 a 12 cm
b 6 cm² *(1 mark for both units)*

5 a 36 cm
b 60 cm² *(1 mark for both units)*

6 A ≐ 6 cm² B = 5 cm² C = 4½ cm² D = 6 cm²

7 7½ m² *(1 mark for units)*

8 21 cm² *(1 mark for units)*

Pages 168–169 Circumference and area of a circle

1 15.7 cm   **2** 25.1 m

3 8 cm   **4** 24.6 cm *(1 mark for units)*

5 25.7 cm   **6** 28.3 cm²

7 19.6 cm² *(1 mark for units)*

8 81π cm²   **9** 50.3 cm²   **10** 21.5 cm²

Pages 170–171 Volume

1 48 cm³   **2 a** 15 cm³ **b** 46 cm²

3 2 cm   **4** 210 cm² *(1 mark for units)*

5 4 cm   **6** 8 cm   **7** 600 cm³ (6 m³)

8 D = 180 cm³, C = 240 cm³, A = 288 cm³,
 B = 625 cm³

9 800 litres *(1 mark for 800 000 cm³ or 0.8 m³)*

10 4 cm

Pages 172–173 Statistics

1 a 卌 ||| and 卌 |
  b 2 and 1   **c** 28 days

2 a Frequencies are 2, 4, 5, 4, 7, 3, 3, 2 *(1 mark for 5 or more frequencies correct)*
  b 7
  c

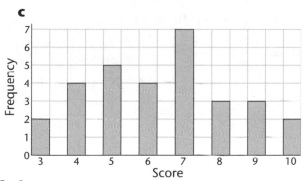

3 3

4 a 6 **b** 12   **5 a** 12 **b** 5

6 a 1 **b** 4

7 a 31 **b** 19 °C **c** 4 °C **d** July, hot

Pages 174–175 Mode, median and mean

1 7   **2** 30

3 a 38 **b** 38 **c** 37.4

4 a 24 **b** 23 **c** 22

5 a 3 **b** 4 **c** 3.9

6 a 30 **b** 2 **c** 57 **d** 1.9

7 a False **b** False **c** True

8 a 10X: 0, 10Y: 4 **b** 10X: 2, 10Y: 2.5
  c 10X: 2.2, 10Y: 2.5
  d 10Y: bigger averages.

Pages 176–177 Comparing distributions

1 B

2 6, 6, 9

3 4, 5, 9

4 2, 8, 8 and 8, 8, 14

5 B more consistent and mode is 0

6 a, b and d

7 a, b and c

8 a both 2.5
  b Aisha 7, Sarah 3
  c Aisha as she sometimes scores lots of goals in one match or Sarah as she is more consistent

9 a i 7 **ii** 7
  b i 10 **ii** 4
  c Outside is more consistent or greenhouse has more tomatoes on some plants

Pages 178–179 Line graphs

1 a 14 °C
  b Thursday and Saturday
  c Friday 17 °C
  d Line has no meaning. Temperature changes throughout the day. Values are just the value at 12 midday.

2 a Midnight 4 °C, Midday 6 °C
  b 6 °C
  c Friday 13 °C

3 a 1900 miles
  b 5500 miles
  c June

4 a About 9500
  b No, still above 5000 and may not drop below
  c Yes, change is continuous, so about 15 000

5 No, can't assume it keeps raining but if depth continues to rise at same rate as between 10 am and 11 am area will flood by 2 pm.

Pages 180–181 Pie charts

1 3 : 1

2 160°, 60°, 140°, 360° *(1 mark for first three)*

3 a Angles: Blue 162°, White 72°, Silver
126° *(1 mark for any two)*

b

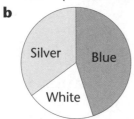

(1 mark if any sector wrong or if not labelled)

4 15   **5** 160

6 40   **7** c   **8** a

9 Angles: British 162°, American 90°,
French 72°, German 36°

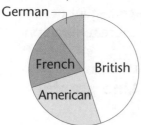

10 Angles: Blue 216°, Silver 108°, Black 36°

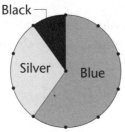

Pages 182–183 Frequency diagrams

1 a 11, 9, 6, 4

b

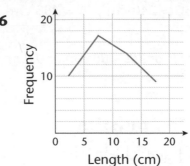

2 a 27   **b** 14   **c** 0, 1 or 2

3 a, b and d

4
```
0 | 7 8 8 8 9
1 | 1 2 3 3 5 7 8 9
2 | 1 2
```

5 a 16   **b** 7   **c** 56   **d** 102

6

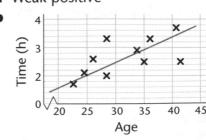

7 a 34   **b** 22   **c** 21 years

Pages 184–185 Scatter diagrams

1 a i W   **ii** N   **iii** K   **iv** G
b i N   **ii** G   **iii** S   **iv** K

2 a

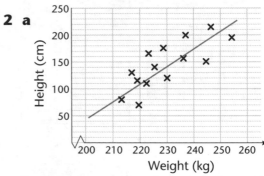

b 150 cm   **c** No, doesn't fit line of best fit.

3 $2\frac{1}{2}$ hours   **4** a, c and d

5 a, b and d

6 a Weak positive

b

c $3\frac{1}{2}$ –4 hours

Pages 186–187 Surveys

1 b and c

2 a i Not enough responses
  ii Not enough responses
  iii Not relevant to question

  b Good range of responses that covers all
  views

3 1 Leading question, 2 offensive question

4 Derek. Others are biased, Derek gets a random sample.

5 Not enough responses

6 Quota sampling, will give a varied sample

7 All the men and only a fraction of women is not representative.

8 a i Not enough responses
ii Not enough responses
iii Not relevant to question
b Good range of responses which can be analysed mathematically

9 Owen. All methods give a random sample but the more pupils surveyed the better.

Pages 188–189 Probability 1

1 $\frac{1}{2}$

2 $\frac{1}{2}$

3

| Impossible | Very unlikely | Unlikely | Evens | Likely | Very likely | Certain |

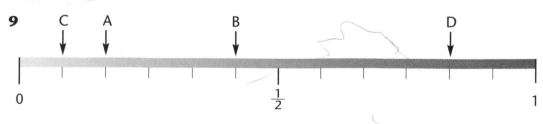

4 a $\frac{3}{5}$ **b** $\frac{2}{5}$

5 a $\frac{7}{10}$ **b** $\frac{3}{10}$

6 $\frac{3}{7}$

7 3

8 $\frac{11}{20}$

9

(1 mark if 3 correct)

10 a $\frac{2}{5}$ **b** $\frac{2}{3}$

Pages 190–191 Probability 2

1 a $\frac{2}{5}$ **b** $\frac{2}{3}$ **2** $\frac{11}{25}$

3 Red 8, Blue 2   **4 a** $\frac{1}{4}$ **b** $\frac{1}{2}$

5 a HHH, HHT, HTH, HTT, THH, THT, TTH, TTT
b $\frac{1}{8}$

6 a $\frac{1}{6}$ **b** $\frac{1}{12}$ **c** $\frac{1}{6}$ **7 a** $\frac{9}{25}$ **b** $\frac{13}{25}$

8 a

		First score		
	1	2	3	4
1	2	3	4	5
2	3	4	5	6
3	4	5	6	7
4	5	6	7	8

Second score

b i $\frac{1}{2}$ **ii** $\frac{3}{16}$ **iii** $\frac{3}{8}$

Pages 192–198 Practice Paper 1 (non-calculator)

Question	Mark	Correct response	Comments
1 a	1	08:03	
b	1	31 min	Work out 08:41 – 08:10
c	1	Doesn't stop, express bus	
2 a	1	48	Work out 100 – 52
b	1	4	Work out 100 ÷ 25
c	1	6	Work out 600 ÷ 100
d	1	30	First work out 35 x 2, then take the answer from 100.
3 a	1	D	
b	1	8	
c	1	8	
4 a	1	8.4 (cm)	Work out 4.2 + 4.2 or 4.2 x 2
	1	5 (cm) or 5.0 (cm)	Work out 2.5 + 2.5 or 2.5 x 2
b	1	6	Find the number of times 2.5 goes into 15, so work out 15 ÷ 2.5
5	1		You can check your answers with a mirror or tracing paper.
	1		For diagonal mirror lines, it is easier to turn the page round until the mirror line is horizontal or vertical.
6	2 or 1	(£)140

Showing a correct method, e.g. (1040 – 200) ÷ 6 | First work out 1040 – 200 = 840 to find the remainder, then each instalment is 840 ÷ 6 = 140 |
7	1	20 (cl)	1 litre = 100 centilitres, 100 ÷ 5 = 20
8 a	1	For example,	Acute angles are less than 90° and obtuse angles are between 90° and 180°.
b	1	An acute angle is less than 90° and four times a number less that 90° must be less than 360°.	This is a Using and Applying maths question. In your answer, you must show that you know the sum of the angles in a quadrilateral is 360°.
9 a	2	80, 60%	Remember that a percentage means out of 100.
b	1	Any that work: 5 out of 100, 1 out of 20, etc.	

10

Question	Mark	Correct response	Comments
10 a	1	$\frac{12}{25}$	Your answers to this question must be written as a fraction. Answers such as 12 out of 25 or 12 in 25 or 12 : 25 are not acceptable.
b	1	$\frac{8}{25}$	
c	1	$\frac{20}{25}$ or $\frac{4}{5}$	20 chocolates are not white. You would not lose the mark if you did not cancel down the fraction.
11	2 or 1	(£)3.75 digits 3375 seen	Use a suitable method to work out 1.35 x 25, which is 33.75. The saving is 33.75 – 30 = 3.75
12 a	1 1	18 19	Work out 6 + (2 x 5) + 2 = 6 + 10 + 2 Work out (3 x 6) + 5 – (2 x 2) = 18 + 5 – 4 = 19
b	1	7	$a + b + c = 13$, so $d = 20 - 13 = 7$
13	1 1 1	$\frac{11}{12}$ $\frac{7}{12}$ $\frac{4}{12}$ or $\frac{1}{3}$	$\frac{1}{2} = \frac{6}{12}$ $\frac{1}{4} = \frac{3}{12}$ and $\frac{1}{3} = \frac{4}{12}$ $\frac{3}{4} = \frac{9}{12}$
14 a	1	<table><tr><td>x</td><td>2</td><td>4</td><td>6</td></tr><tr><td>y</td><td>7</td><td>**9**</td><td>**11**</td></tr></table>	The mapping $y = x + 5$ means add 5 to each x-value to get the y-value.
b	1	<table><tr><td>x</td><td>2</td><td>4</td><td>6</td></tr><tr><td>y</td><td>1</td><td>**5**</td><td>**9**</td></tr></table>	The mapping $y = 2x - 3$ means multiply each x-value by 2 and then subtract 3 to get the y-value.
c	1	$(y) = \frac{1}{2}x + 1$ or $(y) = x \div 2 + 1$	To get the y-value, you halve each x-value and then add 1.
15 a	1	(–3, –2)	
b	1	(–1, 0)	Draw the line AB to find the mid-point.
16 a	2 or 1	Cuboid B	The surface area of a cuboid is the total area of its 6 faces. A = 62 cm², B = 88 cm², C = 82 cm². You would get 1 mark for finding the correct surface area for two cuboids.
b	2 or 1	Cuboid C	The volume of a cuboid is $V = lwh$. A = 30 cm³, B = 40 cm³, C = 42 cm³. You would get 1 mark for finding the correct volume for two cuboids.
c	1	1 (cm)	$V = 10 \times 3 \times h$, so $30 = 30h$ and $h = 1$
17 a	1	No. The sides are the same length, but the 4 angles are not 90°, or it is a rhombus.	
b	1	Yes. Two pairs of adjacent sides have the same length.	

Question	Mark	Correct response	Comments
c	1	No. It only has one pair of parallel sides, or it is a trapezium.	
18	1 1 1	−2 −4 −5	$12 + (−2) = 10$, since +(−) is the same as − $6 − (−4) = 10$, since −(−) is the same as + $−2 × (−5) = 10$, since − x − = +
19	2 or 1	$\frac{1}{4}$ $\frac{6}{24}$ or $\frac{3}{12}$	To multiply fractions, multiply the numerators and the denominators. You would get 1 mark for not cancelling.
20	1 1 1	$(x) = 4$ $(y) = 5$ $(z) = 3$	$2x = 8$ (take 3 from both sides) $x = 4$ (divide both sides by 2) $3y − 6 = 9$ (multiply out brackets) $3y = 15$ (add 6 to both sides) $y = 5$ (divide both sides by 3) $2z − 4 = 2$ (take z from both sides) $2z = 6$ (add 4 to both sides) $z = 3$ (divide both sides by 2)
21 a	1	95 (kg), 12	Interpret the final entry in the diagram for the heaviest person. Count the number of entries in the last 3 rows for those over 70 kg.
b	1	83 (kg), 6	Those over 70 kg are in the last 2 rows.
c	1	76 (kg), 30 (kg)	The modal weight is the weight common to most members. The range is the difference between the heaviest weight and the lightest weight.
22	1 1	$x = 7 − y$ $w = z ÷ 3$ or $\frac{z}{3}$	Take y from both sides to make x the subject. Divide both sides by 3 to make w the subject.

Question	Mark	Correct response	Comments
1 a	1	(£)104.99	Work out 85 + 19.99
b	1	(£)11.02	Work out 2 x 4.49 = 8.98, then 20 – 8.98
c	1	Yes (total is £94.48)	39.99 + 34.50 + 19.99 = 94.48
2 a	1	9	Work out 4 + 5
b	1	The bar should be drawn to 15	Work out what each section on the vertical axis is worth.
c	1 mark for 3 correct	Boys 12 4 Girls 8 4	Boys: 16 ÷ 4 are left handed Girls: 12 ÷ 3 are left handed
3	1 1	Millimetres Kilograms	
4 a	1	24 (cm²)	You can count squares or work out the areas of different squares and rectangles.
b	1 1	8 cm³	The cube is 2 cm by 2 cm by 2 cm. You need to show units if they are not given.
c	1	Any rectangle with correct area	Examples are 2 cm by 12 cm, 3 cm by 8 cm, 4 cm by 6 cm.
5 a	2 or 1	(£)49 Shows a correct method, e.g. 17.5 ÷ 100 x 280	There are many ways of working this out. $17\frac{1}{2}$% of 280 means 17.5 hundredths of 280. This can be calculated by 0.175 x 280 or 17.5 ÷ 100 x 280
b	2 or 1	5(%) Shows a correct method, e.g. 6 ÷ 120 x 100	The fraction is $\frac{6}{120}$ which cancels to $\frac{1}{20}$ You should know that $\frac{1}{20}$ is equivalent to 5%, or you can do the calculation 6 ÷ 120 x 100
6 a	1		All faces of the grey cube must be shaded.
b	2 or 1	For example, For example, 	Any L-shape in any orientation will gain full marks. Any L-shape using 5 cubes in any orientation will gain one mark.

Question	Mark	Correct response	Comments
7 a	2 or 1	30 (people) 12 seen	84° is equivalent to 7 people, so 84 ÷ 7 = 12° is equivalent to 1 person. 360 ÷ 12 = 30
b	2 or 1	162 (degrees) 18 seen	20 people in a pie chart will get 360 ÷ 20 = 18° per person. 9 people will be an angle of 9 x 18 = 162°
8 a	1 1 1	12 or 16 15 17	The factors of 48 are: {1, 2, 3, 4, 6, 8, 12, 16, 24, 48}. You can give both answers. The factors of 150 are: {1, 2, 3, 5, 6, 10, 15, 25, 30, 50, 75, 150}. 'Between' means that you do not include 10 or 20. The factors of 51 are : {1, 3, 17, 51}.
b	1	'No' ticked and an explanation such as '150 is not in the 60 times table.'	You need to make it clear that you understand that a multiple is in the times tables so writing down 60, 120, 180, would just about do this.
9 a	1	110°	Be careful to choose the correct scale on your protractor.
b	2 or 1	250 (metres) 5 cm seen	Multiply the length of *BC* by 50.
10 a	1	12	The range is the difference between the highest and the lowest numbers. From –3 to 9 is a difference of 12.
b	1	20	The total of the negative numbers is –5. The total of the positive numbers is 25. 25 – 5 = 20
c	1	–1	The mode is the most common number.
d	1	1	The median is the middle number when the numbers are in order. These are already in order but there is an even number of values, so the median is midway between 0 and 2.
e	2 or 1	2.5 Showing a correct method, e.g. the total ÷ 8	The mean is the total of the numbers divided by how many numbers there are. The total is 20 and there are 8 values.
11 a	1	23 or 37 or 43 or 47	Prime numbers have no factors other than 1 and themselves. Only one answer is needed but you will not lose the mark if you give more than one.
b	1	25 or 36	Square numbers are numbers that can be written as 5 x 5 or 6 x 6, etc.
c	1	Because square numbers always have a factor other than 1 or itself.	You need to make it clear you know that square numbers can be written as a product such as 2 x 2, 5 x 5, etc.

Question	Mark	Correct response	Comments
12 a	1	75 (degrees)	As the triangle is isosceles, the two base angles are the same. $180 - 30 = 150$, $150 \div 2 = 75$
b	1	135 (degrees)	There are $360°$ in the full turn. The total of the angles shown is $45 + 90 + 90 = 225$. $360 - 225 = 135$
13	3 or 2 or 1	(£)62.50	This is a Using and Applying maths question. You have to convert 1 kg to grams (1000 grams), then divide 1000 by 8 (= 125). You then have to change 125 fifty pence coins into pounds.
		125 seen	
		1000 grams seen	
14 a	2	Any three points on the line.	The possible points are: $(-2, -1)$, $(-1, 0)$, $(0, 1)$, $(1, 2)$, $(2, 3)$, $(3, 4)$, $(4, 5)$, $(5, 6)$.
	or 1	Two points and the corresponding values.	You can read the coordinates from the graph.
b	1	$y = x + 1$	You should see that the second (y) coordinate is equal to 1 more than the first (x) coordinate.
c	1	A line parallel to $y = x + 1$ passing through $(0, 3)$	The line is parallel to the given line but passes through 3 on the y-axis rather than 1.
15	1	1694	Remember to include the bracket keys.
	1	3.5	Work out the numerator and denominator separately first.
16 a	1	219.8 to 220 (cm)	The formula for the circumference is $C = \pi d$ or $C = 2\pi r$.
b	2 or	2200–2300	5 kilometres is 5000 metres which is 500 000cm.
	1	digits 22 or 23 seen	$500\,000 \div (\pi \times 70) = 2273.64$. The answer only has to be approximate, so you can round off.
17 a	1	29.4 (cm)	Work out 21×1.4
b	1	164 (mm)	Work out $229 \div 1.4$
c	1	Yes folded paper is 210 mm x 147 mm	Work out $294 \div 2$ and compare widths and heights.
18	2	Man City by 57 seats (Man Utd 2295, Man City 2352)	Work out $3.4 \div 100 \times 67\,500$ and $4.9 \div 100 \times 48\,000$
19	1	Yes $3 \times (2 \times 18.5 + 13) = 150$, $76 + 4 \times 18.5 = 150$	Substitute $x = 18.5$ in each side of the equation.

Pages 206–207 Mental Mathematics Test

Each question is worth 1 mark each, giving you a total out of 30.

Question	Correct response	Question	Correct response
1	430	20	7
2	3 (m)	21	12 or 16
3	7	22	199
4	–10	23	
5	31		
6	2.25		
7	85 (km)		
8	Friday		
9	Circle		
10	(5, 3)		
11	10		
12	4.5		
13	$\frac{3}{4}$	24	9π (cm^2)
14	33% (33.3%, $33\frac{1}{3}$%)	25	12
15	48 (cm^2)	26	375–425
16	45	27	$x - 4$
17	475 (g)	28	$\frac{1}{3}$
18	0.5 x 0.3 x 0.2	29	Tetrahedron
19	10	30	55

For question 23: